What Others Are Saying...

"Growing Softly Stronger in the Cracked Places offers us a heart opening view of the perfection of all the circumstances of life. Matthew Cox's beautifully written story clearly reminds us that not only do our cracked places - our heart breaking experiences - allow light to shine in the dark night of our soul but these cracks allow us to offer our light, in a more expansive way to the world. And isn't this what the world is asking of each of us right now - to truly live an inspired life in service of a harmonious, just and sustainable human society, or even simply Heaven on Earth?"

Susyn Reeve, author of *The Inspired Life* (Fall 2011)
www.Self-Esteem-Experts.com

"How would you respond when a simple family disagreement turns into an arrest warrant? Would you lash out, become angry, or possibly depressed? Or, would you go within and find a place of peace and contentment while knowing that "all things work together for good." *Growing Softly Stronger in the Cracked Places* chronicles the six weeks of Matthew Cox's life when he learns that freedom isn't about location. It is about perspective. This is a message we all need to hear."

Robert Evans
The Messenger Network

"I have not read an author with such a unique view and insights since Neale Donald Walsch's book, *Conversations with God*. Matthew Cox gives the reader a view inside his deepest thoughts. If you want to expand your mind, stretch the concepts that currently define your life and discover a richness of love and understanding, then this book is for you.

This is an honest and fresh story of struggles and events that happen to a real family and a normal person. How does a "normal" person become incarcerated for hugging their children and still come out of the experience with strong positive feelings? How would anyone react to a sudden arrest, upheaval of a family with 8 children, removal of children from the home, betrayal by extended family, unfounded accusations and indictment? This is a remarkable story of the dramatic events of this family chronicled by a man with the courage to share his story. Open your mind and experience the insights, conclusions and discovery of how the author achieved a phenomenal level of growth, love and understanding for people and events through his journey with the legal system."

Nancy Moureau, PICC Excellence
RN, BSN, CRNI, CPUI, Business Consultant

"A miracle is a shortcut in time and space." So writes author Matt Cox, as he details his experiences behind bars and delves into his own inner space as a means of coping and growing through active loving. Full of hidden gems, this book is a roadmap for well-being; even through the curveballs of life.

Caroline Douglas
Guardian Ad Litem
Co-Author, *New Hampshire Practice Series, Family Law*

Growing Softly Stronger *in the* Cracked Places

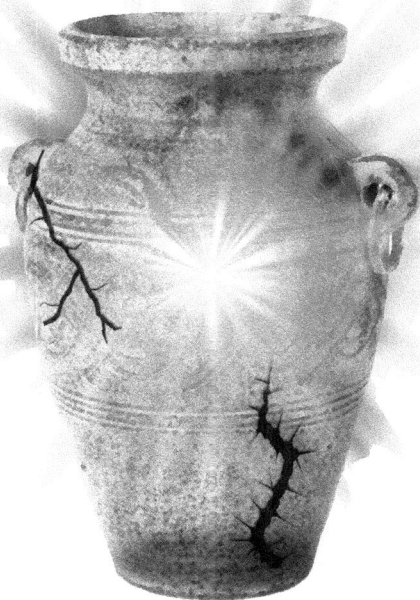

Matthew C. Cox

Growing Softly Stronger in the Cracked Places

First Printing

ISBN 13: 978-0615472102
ISBN 10: 0615472109

Library of Congress Control Number: 2011926566

Published by Peace of Mind Training Institute Publishing

For information contact:

Matthew C. Cox
21 Pine Ridge Road
Sandia Park, NM 87047

This book is dedicated to:

Sheri
Emmanuel
Peter
Mary
Paul
Deborah
Naomi
Esther
Daniel

I love you

Acknowledgements for Softly Stronger

There are a several people who made significant contributions to this project. These include Diana Massengale, who created beautiful artwork and cover design and Stacey Brown, who took over many of my other responsibilities so I could finish this task.

I'm humbled that two distinguished authors, Mim Chapman, Ph.D (www.mimchapman.com) and Alice Ladas Ed.D, stepped in, reviewed this manuscript, and made their own contributions.

I'm especially grateful to Sheri Cox, (The Wife) who has never failed in her belief of our life purpose together and who coordinated this project to bring t to reality.

The number of people who contributed to Growing Softly Stronger in the Cracked Places is beyond my capability to remember or acknowledge. The support and encouragement from each person has shown me how the miraculous is always there, even in the midst of great challenges. I thank each of you for your contribution to those miracles.

Since I have written this as a novel, based on events that happened in my life, you may see yourself in one of the characters in this book. If you recognize yourself and feel my representation of you is unfavorable, please understand that I know you did your best and I am grateful for the influence you had in my story.

A Few Words about This Book

This book is based on actual events. However, because of the outstanding legal issues, our legal counsel has advised me to write it as a novel. Therefore, I have done so. I encourage the reader not to be concerned about the exact truth of each word. Even if I had written this book as non-fiction, the truth would only be truth if it resonated within you. The same is true of a work of fiction. Truth only becomes truth to you once a message speaks to you on a spiritual level. I invite you to allow that voice to speak as you read, without consideration for whether or not the events in this book really happened.

Each character in this book is based upon a real person or a combination of real people However, I have not used their names. Instead, I have used a descriptive title. On the few occasions when I have used a real name, it is because that person is not directly part of this story except as someone who has written or said something worthwhile and I feel they needed to be recognized for this accomplishment.

My intent with this book is not to malign or harm any individual. Instead, it is to make observations about events and developments in such a way that it causes the reader to think and consider where we are going as a community, a society, and a world so that we can change what we need to change as we work together on our individual journeys to Peace of Mind.

Introduction

In today's quest for spiritual enlightenment, it is possible we are doing the exact opposite of what we need to do to reach our spiritual goals and to make a significant impact on our society, our world, our governments. Of course, we are repeating what our predecessors have done. We recognize the truth. We compare it with current ideology. We see the contrast and we shudder at the task in front of us, knowing that if we proclaim the truth too loudly, there may be consequences, painful consequences.

Therefore, instead of facing life directly, we approach it through art. Musicians, painters, sculptures, writers, and performers proclaim the truth in abstract ways, providing clues that resonate with those who hold a common belief and amuse those who don't. While these clues are encouraging to fellow truth seekers, they do little to improve society. The reason is simple. Those clues, as powerful as they are, don't tell the complete message. Many messengers are afraid that if the true message appears, they will be persecuted for their beliefs.

Throughout history, some people have stepped forward to communicate their message They knew that the attention and public debate generated by their message would better society so they took the chance, lived their lives, communicated their truth. In many cases, this was not a conscious decision made by each messenger. Instead, a series of events propelled an individual to the forefront and the individual took the newfound attention as a God-ordained opportunity to do their part.

Ralph Waldo Emerson was one of those individuals. He used his writing and speaking to communicate his truths and he understood the significance of God's design. He grasped the function of nature and the soul. He recognized the uniqueness of each element of our world. He summarized his understanding in a simple quote. "There is a crack in everything God has made."

If Emerson is correct, and I believe he is, I have several ways I can respond to the cracked places in my life. I can attempt to cover the cracked places so that they remain and others can't see them. I can fill in the cracked places with something other than myself so that I pretend to be something I am not. I can accept the cracked places and be as God designed me.

Before I determine which option is best, there are many things to consider. Do my cracked places mean God made a mistake? Do they mean I am somehow flawed? Do they demonstrate a weakness that must be overcome? Or, do they mean that God is perfect, that I am not flawed, and that my cracked places give me clues about my life purpose, my dreams, my goals, my passion?

The logical answer is obvious. God is perfect. Therefore, if God made me with cracked places, that design is perfect. Furthermore, if I cover, fill in, or remove the cracked places, as some philosophies teach, I take away from God's perfect design.

Since God made me with cracked places, the next thing to consider is God's purpose for doing this. Leonard Cohen's song *Anthem* says "That's how the light gets in." If I apply that thought to my spiritual journey, it is reasonable to believe that my cracked places give me clues to my life purpose, my dreams, my goals, my passion. In addition, by accepting, understanding, and strengthening my cracked places, I gain the opportunity to face the fear and emotional pain of what, on the surface, appears to be a flaw.

Because cracked places are different from the norm, some people think cracked places are ugly. Therefore, many philosophies and religions create ugly terms for them. Terms like sin, mistakes, accidents, wrecks, sickness, and disability flood these idea schools with negative connotations and produce emotional and spiritual baggage that discourages individuals from considering that cracked places are to be cherished, celebrated, and even strengthened. The differences of cracked places may make others uncomfortable. However, that doesn't make cracked places evil, bad, or destructive. In fact, those differences highlight an individual's message and give it attention, life, and meaning.

It is only when my cracked place is brought out from under cover, cleared of the filler, and exposed for everyone to see, that I can move forward with my life purpose, dreams, goals, and passion. When I understand this truth, I can openly explore my apparent flaw and recognize it as God's special gift to assist me in sharing the message God wants me to share with others.

In other words, cracked places aren't just for allowing the light to get in. They also allow the light to get out!

This is a book about how my cracked places were put on center stage for everyone to see. I, like the artists I mentioned earlier, was content to be on the sideline, living my life, offering clues, and not making much of an impact on the world. I allowed the light of truth into my life and explored new ideas. I communicated them to a small following of people via blog posts, seminars, and a book read by a couple dozen people.

Then, through an experience of emotional pain, fear of loss, and betrayal, I became someone literally on trial for being different. The cracked places that allowed light into my life suddenly glowed with an intensity that could no longer be ignored by those on the outside. In response to my situation, I decided to clean out my cracked places and put them on full display. In doing so, I experienced outstanding challenges and phenomenal miracles that would not have been possible otherwise. By reading this book, you may share in those experiences.

The reader may be wondering what a cracked place is so before I conclude this introduction, I will offer you an example. One of my cracked places is "integrity." Don't misunderstand me. I don't have difficulty with integrity. I practice it relentlessly. I always have. Integrity is at the core of everything I do. I study it, I read about it, and I teach it. This is a normal thing for a philosopher/writer/teacher to do. However, I go overboard with my efforts. I obsess about it. On the surface, this may not seem like a cracked place but, I assure you, it is.

I see integrity as a complete alignment of thoughts, words, actions, and habits to accomplish a specific task. I practice integrity so relentlessly in my belief system that I won't settle for simplistic explanations that work part of the time and don't work part of the time. Many spiritual leaders fall into catch phrases such as "God is all powerful but the devil is powerful too," "God's ways are above man's ways," and "Sometimes you just got to have faith" to explain the unexpected challenges that happen. These teachings create a weak and schizophrenic God who is all powerful and yet, has no power at all.

I understand there is a God, a Divine Force, a Divine Providence that is Love, Life, and Creation. (For simplicity sake, I refer to this as God. You may know this as God, Goddess, the Universe or another sacred term. I suggest that you substitute your term whenever I use the word "God" in my book.) God always has my best interests in mind. God's thoughts and plans are trustworthy. I never have to be concerned about God punishing me, judging me, or doing anything other than loving me as I explore my life. God always practices complete integrity. There is no contradiction in God's thoughts, words, and actions.

God knows all and therefore exists both inside and outside of the time dimension. That doesn't mean God controls what I perceive to be the future. Since each individual is linked with God, each of us is a co-creator of that future. My part in co-creation is to do what I can do, control what I can control. God's part is to coordinate events so that they assist me in my creation - possibly by giving me an unexpected challenge that seems to take me away from the way I want to go when it actually takes me forward faster than I could have gone through any other method.

This is what happens when I practice integrity, God sees that I am ready to take the next step and orchestrates a series of events that fast-forwards my life and moves me deeper into my life purpose, my dreams, my goals, and my passion. The speed cleans out the cracked places, makes them stronger, and allows the light to get out. At first, this seemed scary to me. Then, as I lived in the middle of the situation, I realized that God is gentle. I realized that since God had prepared me for this situation I didn't need violence, struggle, or pain to grow stronger. I only had to live the experience and allow God to grow me *softly stronger in the cracked places.*

A city on a hill cannot be hidden. Neither do people light a lamp and put it under a bushel. Instead, they put it on its stand, and it gives light to everyone in the house.

In the same way, let your light so shine before men that they may see your good works and praise the beliefs which have sponsored them.

By this means, you can help others span the chasm between yesterday and tomorrow, and close the gap between the comfort of tradition and the necessity of innovation.

The New Revelations
Neale Donald Walsch

Growing Softly
Stronger *in the*
Cracked Places

Wednesday, December 8, 2010

I have now been arrested twice.

The first was a miracle without logical or reasonable explanation. The second time was equally miraculous and much more intense. I'm grateful for the first arrest because it prepared me for the second.

The second arrest, which is the catalyst for this book, took place today, Wednesday, December 8, 2010. The Wife and I willingly went to the sheriff's office to discuss our parenting skills and start the process of returning our three youngest kids back to our home.

After several hours of separate interviews with a nervous detective, The Bernalillo County Sheriff's Office arrested each of us on 45 counts of identical charges.

For me, the interview process was a fascinating observation about how a person acts when under stress. Yes, I experienced some stress during the process; however, I had spent the previous few months learning to stay in the moment by using ancient breathing techniques. The detective was another story. He fidgeted, lied, contradicted himself, and demonstrated all the body language of a kid explaining his way out of something he shouldn't have been doing.

By the end of our time together, I began to feel sorry for him. His job placed him in a position where he had to be suspicious to advance his career. I wondered if he would ever trust another person, including himself.

Upon arrest, we were searched, handcuffed, and taken across the street to the transport center. It was then that I realized that we could be a huge media story. I kept my head down, watching my steps, not looking for a TV camera. My five years of radio experience wrote the headline. "Parents arrested for 45 abuse charges." I could hear the story in my head and realized nothing would be a secret anymore.

Immediately, I reminded myself that there is no such thing as bad PR (public relations) and that all attention is good attention. I would have to write a book. I smiled slightly at the thought and that eased the knot in the pit of my stomach.

I was searched the second time as the officers inventoried my clothing and moved me into holding. I proudly navigated the use of the restroom after they moved my cuffs from behind me to in front of me. I say proudly because I've always had something of a bashful kidney. I got over that during my first arrest, so the difficulty here was just manipulating the plumbing while wearing handcuffs.

With the deed done, the officer moved the cuffs behind me and put me by myself in a holding cell. Throughout the long day, I had distracted myself with numerous meditation techniques until this time. Now, I took time to consider my options. There weren't many. We'd be transported to the Metropolitan Detention Center (MDC) on the west side of Albuquerque. We'd be given a bond to pay and we could be free. I knew there was a possibility of a large bond. I wondered how big it would be.

A few weeks earlier, one of my accounting clients received a $500,000 cash only bond. Would I match that? The Revolutionary is an amazingly talented man. He came to me in the spring of 2009 with an accounting issue that was really a relationship issue. I was able to help him with both. His partners were so impressed with me that they became my clients on other matters.

After that issue was settled, The Revolutionary almost hired The Wife and me to do coaching with him and the mother of his child. I say almost because after he made the first payment, she refused to attend the session and I refunded the money.

The next time I heard The Revolutionary's name he was the accused killer of a friend. They had argued, The Revolutionary stepped outside to cool off and his friend followed. They fought. The Revolutionary, being the bigger man, won by knockout. Someone found his hurt friend by the roadside, called an ambulance, and his friend died on the way to the hospital.

In spite of what appeared to be obvious facts, part of me felt like The Revolutionary had been set up. He was involved in radical anti-government organizations and he was good at it. He used the internet and rallies to communicate his message. He was afraid of the government and that fear motivated him to attempt to hide. I surmised he might have other, specific reasons to stay out of the governments' line of sight but I had no facts to prove it.

The contradiction with ¯he Revolutionary was that even though he took outrageous steps to hide, he often did things to put himself in the spotlight. He successfully led a huge political rally, did radio shows, and now, he was an accused murderer.

The transportation officers arrived and led me from my cell through a narrow hallway, out a back door, towards the van. We used to call them paddy wagons taking "fresh meat" to jail. Now, The Wife and I were the fresh meat, squeezing into seats on opposite sides of the van. The van was split lengthwise with two benches running front to back, separated by a metal divider. I slid to the front and two other prisoners slid in behind me. I had learned during my first arrest to hang on to the seatbelt behind me so I wouldn't slide. I thought it was funny that we weren't buckled to the seats. Albuquerque has a seatbelt law, but it doesn't apply to those in custody.

I laid back my head while everyone finished loading. I could hear The Wife's voice on the other side of the van. It was muted by the divider, but I was sure it was her. I wondered how often I would hear her voice over the next few weeks. The officers got into the front of the van and the passenger asked the driver if he was ready to go. Upon receiving an affirmative reply, he told the driver to "keep it under 90."

The transport was uneventful. The other two males talked about their arrest and asked me about mine. They complained about the length of the trip and wondered where we were going. One seemed to be a Mexican national who kept talking about leaving "fucking America." The other had been picked up on an outstanding traffic warrant.

We arrived at the facility, unloaded and were un-cuffed. I was grateful. Handcuffs are uncomfortable at best, painful at worst and I had managed this encounter without bruises or scrapes.

Processing required us to sit with six guys shackled and chained together who were being extradited from California to Texas. Some of them had slept outside the night before during the extradition process. They took turns going to the bathroom while they told stories about how they were caught, where they ate, and how they traveled. They left processing to continue their trip before we did.

We signed our property inventory sheet and completed the medical questionnaire. However, unlike my last arrest, no one reviewed my charges or told me my bond amount. I knew that mean a bond amount had not yet been set. I realized this might not be a quick process.

Once we were through with processing, it was time to move into MDC's temporary holding. For the third time since my arrest, I was patted down. This time the guard searched my mouth, handled my ball sack, and made me take off my shoes.

Once through the door, I was directed down the hall to Cell 5 in the corner of temporary holding. I took three steps and the gal at the desk told me to stand against the wall. This was my next clue that this wasn't going to be a quick process.

During my previous arrest, I had only been in Cell 5, a 20x20 concrete room with a toilet behind a half wall in the corner and a cement bench along the walls. There were 35 men jammed into that space the last time, most of them sleeping off a Friday night drunk.

Today, I stood against the wall and waited... and waited. Waiting is something that happens a lot after an arrest. There is no hurry to get anything done. I could only remain in the moment, watch my breath, and calm my mind. Otherwise, a person could go crazy.

Eventually, I was taken to a changing room where I stripped and was told to squat and cough in case I was "keistering" contraband. Then, I was handed orange pants and a matching top with "MDC JAIL INMATE" stenciled on the back. I put them on and realized I was, for the first time in my life, an official jail inmate. During my first time in jail, I had not changed out of my own clothes so I felt like I was just visiting. The orange suit made this feel much different.

With my change complete, I was escorted to a two-way TV to answer some questions. The girl on the screen told me I had court scheduled the next day at 1:30 and my bond would be set then.

I asked if I could make a phone call and was told I could later. Then I was sent to Cell 3 and put there by myself. On the way through, I noticed The Wife was also in a cell by herself on the female side of temporary holding.

Cell 3 was a 6x10 room with a concrete bench that was 5' 9" long. A half wall ended the bench and hid the toilet in the corner making it difficult for me to stretch out my 6 foot frame on the bench. I did the best I could to make myself comfortable and attempted to sleep.

My tummy grumbled and I realized I hadn't eaten since breakfast 12 hours earlier. The hunger and stress of the day curled me into a ball and I turned to my side to sleep.

I was awakened once to answer some questions and have my picture taken. I was given my inventory list. It was the only thing in the world that was mine. Everything else had been removed from my presence. I was awakened a second time to talk with a mental health counselor. The Mental Health Counselor was young, inexperienced, mostly unprofessional, and scared. She wore a huge fake diamond ring and asked me a series of mental health questions similar to the ones asked earlier that day in processing. We were interrupted by her phone, her radio, and a visitor at the door. At the completion of each interruption, she had to ask me "where were we?" I was grateful at least one of us was paying attention.

With the questioning complete, The Mental Health Counselor made a grand announcement. "Because of the nature of your charges, I cannot guarantee your safety in this facility. Therefore I'm putting you in administrative segregation in one of our psych wards." I let the words sink in and told her I understood.

I went back to Cell 3 for a few more minutes. Then, I was finger printed and allowed to make my phone call. It was after 10:00, past the bedtime of all my kids except Daughter One. Daughter One is married and has two kids. I assumed she would be up with the baby and I was right.

During the brief phone call, I learned that my arrest was big news. At least two people had contacted Daughter One volunteering to be character witnesses after seeing the story on TV. I also learned that the sheriff's office confiscated our computers, including our network drives and backups. I had told Daughter One and the other children how to run the business if I was away for a while. I had never considered what to do if they didn't have business data to use.

I ran out of time on the phone and the guard told me to grab two blankets and shoved a sack lunch in my hands. He escorted me to a sally port and I noticed that The Wife was no longer in temporary holding. I wondered when I would see her again.

The Wife and I have been married since January 1, 1986. With 2011 on the horizon, we decided to watch the ball drop in Times Square for our 25th wedding anniversary. Now, I wondered if that planned and paid-for trip would happen. In fact, with the day's events, I wondered if anything I had spent the past building would happen.

I started building in 1984 when I attended a seminar led by Bill Gothard. Mr. Gothard had an influence on my early life and I still recognize the wisdom in teachings. While there, I received a vision of fifty people in three generations to make the world a better place through bringing peace. I saw the possibility of eight children, their mates, and an average of four kids for each couple. I really didn't know how it would happen, or even if the family would be biological but, over the years, the fifty people in three generations never wavered.

I met The Wife later that year and she loved my vision. She's a natural helper who has the ability to throw herself into any task as if it is hers. I've learned over the years that she isn't really helping me with my vision as much as she is fulfilling hers. I still remember the day she first heard about my vision and said, "It sounds good to me."

Our vision has moved steadily forward since then. Son One and Son Two were born in February 1987. Son One is the first born, although we suspect Son Two was the first conceived. Son Two weighed 1.5 pounds more than Son One at birth and looked older. (Yes, twins can be conceived at different times, during different menstrual cycles. There are even recorded instances of twins having different fathers.)

Son Two went through some challenging relationships several years ago and decided to come back and commit strongly to helping the family. He's a rock who has a unique understanding of the spiritual realm.

Son One has been consistent in his life, doing whatever is needed. Over the last year, he began a relationship with a young lady and they are expecting a child in March. Now, she wants to move to Illinois to be closer to her family instead of being here. He is torn between fulfilling his family commitments to us and fulfilling them to her.

The choice to go with her seems obvious until you understand that, two years ago, we all agreed to use the next 3-5 years to pay off family debt. With the debt gone, our revenue stream would be able to help everyone get established in their own homes. Son One's Partner, knew this when she began the relationship with him. Still, she's insistent on pulling him away. I understand why she's doing it. However, that doesn't mean I like it or agree with it.

Daughter One was born in November 1988. She married Daughter One's Partner in 2008 and they have two kids, Grandchild One and Grandchild Two. Daughter One is outspoken, deeply feels her emotions, and is intuitive. She helps me with my accounting practice and serves as a litmus test for my ideas.

The other five kids are Son Three, born in 1990, Daughter Two, 1992; Daughter Three, 1994; Daughter Four 1996; and Son Four, 1998. Four boys, four girls; each one is a gift unique to us and vital to our family.

Our family works together, plays together, and learns together. Besides my accounting business, we have a mobile detailing business. In spite of the recent "poor economy," our businesses have thrived over the past two years. They had to thrive for us to survive because our previous business failures had left us with a million dollars in debt. We righted the ship in 2009 and were on pace to pay off more than $60,000 in debt in 2010, until the arrests.

Now, my family was falling apart. I couldn't make money while behind bars, and I couldn't help my kids make money because the computers were confiscated. The detail business could still operate, but December is the slowest month of the year and, without the computers, they couldn't run credit cards.

Fortunately, a hail storm had blown through the area on October 2 doing costly cosmetic damage to our cars, our house, and the next door rental. The roofer was supposed to start on our roof the day after our arrest. During my brief phone call, I told Daughter One to postpone the repair in the anticipation that we would need the insurance money for legal expenses.

I went through the sally port in silence, hugging my blankets and sack lunch. The guard escorted me down a series of halls and through another sally port into PAC-2. This POD would be my home for the next part of my adventure. To my left were two cells and beyond them, the Commanding Officer (CO) Station. Opposite the station, along the far wall were a series of bunks. To the right of them were common toilets, urinals, and showers. The room widened from the narrow entrance into a large commons area. The right wall was lined with ten cells. I was led to Cell number 9.

Number 9 was a 7x14 cubicle with a metal desk, a stainless steel toilet/sink unit, and a metal shelf for a bed. I threw the blankets on the bed, the lunch, and inventory list on the desk, and surveyed my situation. I was hungry and I didn't have an appetite. As the door locked behind me, I looked into the bag to discover two pieces of white bread, a slice of bologna, and a slice of processed "cheese." I nibbled on the meat and left the rest. I decided to sleep.

I put one blanket on the bare metal and crawled on top of it. I pulled the other one over me and lay on my back. My hips were already sore from laying on the concrete downstairs in Cell 3, so sleeping on my side wasn't an option. I slept on my back for about half an hour until I was awakened by keys in my door as the CO called my name and said, "Here's a mattress." I rejoiced, pulled the three inches of vinyl wrapped padding on the metal shelf, and remade my bed. This time, I folded one of the blankets into a pillow and used the other one for warmth.

During the night, I alternated between sleep and meditation, trying to find a comfortable position for my body and my mind. By morning, I had made significant progress releasing attachment to my life of the previous day and moving into the flow of my current experience.

Thursday, December 9, 2010

This skill of moving into the flow of life, without resistance, is one I have taught for several years. Nature teaches us that wind, water, fire, and earth must flow to be healthy. When something blocks the flow, constipation occurs that must be corrected or death will ensue. The unblocking can often be dramatic and painful, especially if the resistance is persistent.

I recognized that my current situation was an excellent opportunity to resist. It was painful. I could lose everything I had built over the past 26 years. My family, my business, and my possessions could all disappear as a result of this situation. I released them, all of them. I could do nothing else and remain within the integrity of my belief system.

This was not a minor event. I went through the process of detaching from each thing that was a part of my life just twenty-four hours earlier. I don't know how long this process took. I just knew I had to do it. I had no way of knowing if or when I would ever see The Wife or any of our children again. I did not know how any of my friends, family, and clients would respond to my arrest. I recognized that I could lose everything that was important to me so I emotionally released it all. At that time, I became a single, childless, friendless pauper.

My sleep was interrupted during the early morning hours by various noises. The POD TV played for several hours. The POD telephone rang with the first three notes of the ESPN

SportCenter theme song – Da Da Dat! The beeping of the sally port door, the jiggling of keys as the CO made his regular rounds, the conversations between guards as they gave each other breaks, and the toilets all combined to create a hushed cacophony of sound.

The high pressure toilets of MDC make a quick rushing sound when flushed. Then, once the water leaves the bowl, it creates a vacuum to suck in clean water. This refilling produces a sound similar to the blowing of a conch shell. I wondered if anyone could sleep through the sound. Every time someone flushed during the night, the sound echoed off the concrete block walls and resounded through the POD.

My fitful sleep was interrupted when the CO unlocked the door and a gentleman, dressed in orange, handed me breakfast. I thought it odd that a fellow inmate would be serving meals but I thanked him and sat down to eat. Breakfast was powdered eggs, bologna, and something I couldn't identify. I ate what I recognized, left the rest, and put the tray along with last night's sack lunch by the door. I assumed someone would pick it up and they did.

There was nothing to do so I went back to bed, again alternating between sleep and meditation. I had reached a sense of peace and I wanted to maintain it. Sometime later – after an hour, maybe two, I heard someone say "nine please" and I heard my door unlock. I got up to see the same man that served me breakfast greeting me with a broom and dustpan.

"I'm a mentor on this POD. I need you to sweep your cell then, put the trash into your toilet."

The Monk had grey hair, a beard, gentle eyes, and a soothing voice. I liked him immediately. I did as instructed, traded the broom for a mop, and mopped my cell. With my chores done for the day, I climbed back into bed. I had nothing to read, nothing to write with, nothing to do at all. I practiced staying in the moment, watching my breath, and just being. I wondered how long I'd have to do this.

"Do the Tibetan Rites."

The voice in my head was clear and I knew I had to respond. I had done the exercise routine every day since June 1 and I had just enough room in my cell to do it here. The routine, a series of five calisthenics, each performed 21 times with a short breathing exercise in between had been part of my physical and spiritual meditation ever since I committed to do it for ninety straight days. I fulfilled my commitment on August 31 and decided to continue it indefinitely.

I was fascinated by how my body responded to it each day. It taxed my primary and secondary muscles, producing the wonderful soreness associated with muscle growth. The slight pain rotated from my legs to my arms to my chest to my shoulders to my abs. With most exercise routines, my body would plateau and figure out shortcuts so that I no longer benefitted. With The Five Tibetan Rites (TFT), I couldn't find that plateau and my body continued to adjust to it. In fact, I noticed even greater benefit after my initial 90 day commitment.

I stood up, moved my blankets to the desk, and began. I circled 21 times then, moved to the breathing exercise. I used my cot to do leg lifts, followed again by the breathing exercise. Then, I did the backward bend, breathing exercise, reverse table, breathing exercise, up dog, down dog and the final breathing exercise. I knew many people got into great shape when in jail. I decided to be one of them. I would grow stronger spiritually, physically, and mentally.

With the rites done, I again went back to bed. I was aware of movement within the POD. There was some kind of group meeting and discussion group. I assumed I would never be a part of that life because I was in administrative segregation. I steeled myself to enjoy me and to tie into my spiritual side as a way to maintain my sanity. This would be me, myself, and I and we would be fine.

My sleep and meditation ritual was interrupted by PAC 2 Psychiatrist, who opened my door and introduced herself as the staff psychiatrist. She apologized for waking me. I explained that I taught seminars on how to have Peace of Mind and I was practicing what I taught. She smiled and asked me questions about my mental state. In response to each question, I told her I wasn't angry, didn't feel like hurting anyone else or feel like harming myself. She asked if I needed anything and I asked for reading material. She got Doctor's Son, who was a fellow inmate and another mentor in the POD.

Doctor's Son had deep emery skin and penetrating eyes, eyes that wanted to connect with those around him and eyes that were afraid to do so. PAC 2 Psychiatrist relayed my request to Doctor's Son and he agreed to find me something to read.

"What do you want to read?"

I told him I wanted a self-help book or maybe a "sports novel." I don't know that I've ever used those two words in the same sentence before. It seemed funny to me, even as they came out of my mouth. However, within a few minutes, Doctor's Son was back with *Squeeze Play*, by Jane Leavy described on the cover by Entertainment Weekly as "the best sports novel ever written."

I thanked him for his help as the door locked behind him.

The book was cold water to a parched throat. Meditation is a powerful tool and I use it daily to gain direction and clarity. In addition, I believe that outside stimuli carry messages for me too. Reading is my preferred "outside stimuli" and I was grateful for the book. I read for I don't know how long until I was interrupted by someone unlocking my door. This time, it was Officer S.

"Aren't you going to take your time out? It's time for lunch?"

I told her I didn't know I was allowed out of my room.

"Who told you that?"

"I was told that during processing."

"Why did they tell you that?"

"They said I had a high profile case and I had to stay in the cell for my own protection. "

"Let me check on something."

S left my door unlocked and walked to the COs desk while I returned to my bunk and read. She was slightly overweight and had a beautiful smile. I decided she was a very kind CO. In fact, she was to become my fourth angel experience of the day.

I believe angels come in many forms and fashions. They influence and help us every day. We often don't see them because we aren't paying attention. In my current situation, my "angel eyes" were on full alert.

My first angel experience of the day came between breakfast and chores. I was on my bunk, facing the wall, somewhere between asleep and awake when I felt pressure on my shoulder and lower back. Somebody or something was touching me with outstretching hands. I was suddenly very awake and I turned around to see nothing, absolutely nothing. I knew immediately that someone was sending me love.

Later that morning, I opened my eyes and saw a neon green glow in the room. The glow was consistent in size with the being that touched me earlier. I was reminded of the Biblical stories of men in prison that were visited by angels. In some cases, the angels helped the people escape. In other cases, they just provided comfort. I knew immediately that the angels were not there to help me escape. They were there to help me be free.

Angel number 3 was The Monk, the mentor I met earlier, and angel number 4 was S. She returned to my cell and told me that I did have serious charges. However, I also had the right to be out of my cell. I could eat my lunch, shower, make phone calls, and even go outside to the recreational area. She gave me a hygiene kit so that I could brush my teeth and take a shower. For the first time, I wandered out of my cell, roamed the POD, took a shower, and watched my back.

After my shower, S pulled me aside and told me I was safe in this POD. She said many of the inmates were so sedated by medication that they wouldn't be able to harm me even if they could comprehend my situation. She pointed out The Vulture and explained that he couldn't even remember her name. She had me watch other inmates and notice the glaze in their eyes. I realized she was telling me the truth.

I attempted to use the telephone and discovered a system that was both frustrating and inadequate. There were two ways to make a phone call: collect and with a debit card. It seemed that collect calls to an inmate's family were blocked. Therefore, I could only call with a debit card. Debit cards were available through the center's commissary. Commissary orders were placed on Wednesday, to arrive on Thursday. Today was Thursday. Therefore, it would be a week before I could make a call to my family because I had arrived after the order deadline

I felt lonely and isolated. I'd figuratively been hit in the gut again and again over the past 24 hours. My emotional strength was zapped and I was physically weak. I centered myself and started to self-talk about maintaining strength. I decided to go for a walk in the sun.

The POD's outdoor recreational area was a triangle about 60 x 60 x 40. It had 20 foot high concrete walls on two sides and glass on the side that faced the pod. Fencing covered the top of the area so that the sky looked like a mosaic of blue with black lines. I quickly realized that the area was on the south side of the POD. Therefore, we received maximum winter sunshine exposure. I was grateful.

My walk was interrupted by several fellow inmates as they came outside to play handball. I noticed faded lines on the floor and walls so I stepped aside and stood in the sunshine to watch. The Monk was playing and he invited me to play. I accepted and carefully learned the rules of the court as two others joined us for doubles. The games were lively, competitive, and polite. I held my own even though my arms and legs felt like lead weights.

We played for almost an hour and then came inside. The other inmates wanted to get showers before the noon towel turn in deadline and I needed to get ready for court. At this point, I realized time is different in MDC. Breakfast arrives early, sometimes as early as 3:30. (I learned later that the early breakfast was designed to accommodate inmates who had to be at court by 8:30. Those who weren't going to court would receive early breakfast and go back to bed for two-three hours.) Lights come on a little after 7 and lunch arrives around 10, sometimes as early as 9. Dinner arrives between 4 and 6. I was to learn that the timing of the meals were important to my time out of the cell and to the social culture of MDC. I was often allowed out of my room to eat lunch and dinner, and allowed to remain out until the next lockdown. Otherwise, I remained in my cell.

As I started to step into my cell and continue reading, I heard my name over the POD intercom. A representative from the public defender's office was there to see me. She introduced herself and began to ask questions about my income. She quickly determined that I made too much money for their free services and told me they would be in touch about how I could hire their office to represent me. I knew I wanted to hire a private attorney so I told her I probably wouldn't need their services. She asked me if I had any phone numbers for attorneys and I told her I didn't. She promised she would find one for me and mentioned a person I had never heard of who had worked with high profile cases like mine.

She continued and said that, for today, they had to represent me and she asked me what I could afford for bail. Since I knew this was a negotiation process, I gave her a low number. She told me she didn': think that was enough for my charges, but she would "see what she could do" and she would see me in court.

I headed back into my cell and again heard my name over the POD intercom. I put my head out the door and noticed two men from Light and Liberty Jail Ministry were visiting the POD. One waved at me and I went out to meet him. The Preacher introduced himself and told me The Father-in-Law had sent him.

The Father-in-Law is The Wife's dad. Our youngest three kids had stayed with him and The Mother-in-Law for the past three weeks after someone had reported us for suspected child abuse. I was sure The Father-in-Law was heartbroken at what he thought had happened in our family. I'm also sure he saw this as God's way of punishing us because he thought we had turned our back on God when we stopped attending traditional Christian church services.

The truth was that we had discovered a spirituality that allowed us to connect to God in a way that didn't need organized religion. Without the confines of traditional religion, I felt and saw God's hand in greater ways than ever before. The punishment of The Father-in-Law's current belief system and my old belief system was no longer one of those ways for me, especially for a God who is love. I braced myself to hear a message of repentance from The Preacher and decided to be friendly and gracious.

The Preacher asked how I was doing and I told him I had made good progress over the past few hours. I told him my angel stories. I quoted Romans 8:28 "...all things work together for good" and we had a nice conversation. He gave me a Bible and it was time for court.

My escort to court had a partner and that partner was escorting The Wife. We couldn't talk but at least we could see one another. They led us to MDC's courthouse which was connected by close circuit TV to the downtown courthouse. We had seen the other side of the system the last time we were arrested. Today, we saw this side.

The Wife and I chatted briefly before court started. The public defender's representative slipped me a yellow sticky note with the promised attorney's name and number and I told The Wife I would attempt to contact him. I had also thought about the attorney we used for our previous case. She was inexpensive and adequate but contacting her for this situation didn't feel right.

Before court began, I had thirty seconds to chat with the appointed public defender about our terms of release. I had two trips planned during the 60-day period when we would normally be required to stay in New Mexico. In addition, we needed a low bond so we could get out and serve my clients who had given me payroll and payroll tax payment responsibilities.

Court started and my case and The Wife's case were identical. The district attorney's representative recommended a $250,000 cash bond and the public defender argued for a lower, more reasonable bond. The judge set the bond at $500,000 cash. In most cases, a bond is cash or surety and an inmate can get out for 10% of the stated amount, therefore an inmate with a $100,000 bond may bail out for $10,000. We did not have this kind of bond. Each of our bonds was cash only. We would need a million cash to leave the facility. We didn't have access to that kind of cash. We had about $10,000 in the bank and I knew another $8,000 would arrive soon. I also knew that some bail bond companies would take payments but I could think of no way for us to work through this situation.

In addition, the judge gave the district attorneys' office the usual ten business days to indict us. The deadline for this was December 23.

Immediately after court. The Wife and I were given the opportunity to make phone calls in an effort to tell someone, anyone about our situation. When no one answered our phone calls, we were hustled out of the courtroom lobby and back down the hall to our respective PODs. The only thing I had to help me was the sticky note from the public defender's office with an attorney's name I didn't know.

I have learned over the years that making decisions can be simple or complex. Complex decisions come from a lack of clarity. Jail provides lots of clarity because the choices are limited. MDC sets a schedule and I get to follow it. The only choice I have is to complain or be content. There is little opportunity to plan because most external choices are removed.

Truthfully, this isn't much different from life outside of jail. The Universe has an orchestrated plan for our benefit and we can flow with it or resist it. If we flow with it, stay awake, and welcome it, every day is a day full of miracles and love. If we resist it, the perception of the experience is different.

The Wife and I were escorted back to our PODs and I arrived to find us still under the 2-4 pm lockdown. By the time I was let out of my cell, it was too late to call the recommended attorney. I would have to wait until the next day. I spent the rest of the day reading and trying not to think about being in jail until at least Christmas Eve.

Friday December 10, 2010

Administrative Segregation at MDC has pros and cons. The pros are that I get a private room, out of the general population. If I have reading material and writing tools, the time passes quickly. There is tap water to drink and facilities to use. There is enough room to work out and the temperature is comfortable. The cons are that I never know when I'll be let out into the general population so I can shower, attempt to make a phone call, and interact with other inmates. Of course, this lack of control allows me to free the planning part of my mind. This has taken some adjusting.

My life outside of jail consisted mostly of business ideas, strategies, managing money, marketing, business coaching, and conducting seminars. I explored spirituality within my business life and every exploration caused me to crave a time in the future when I could spend less time on the business aspects and more time on the spiritual connection. I thought this time would happen after we had reached certain financial goals. Once there, I would write, ponder, meditate, and explore deeper spiritual ideas.

I was beginning to understand that this time was now. I remembered my lesson from the previous day about limited choices. I couldn't participate in business activities. I couldn't communicate with the people I usually communicated with. I could accept the reality of my current situation and make the

25

best of it or I could complain. With the outside activity falling away, I determined to turn inside through reading, meditation, and writing. I would make this time a spiritual retreat.

I knew I wasn't the first person to do this and I could think of no better way to spend my time.

Today went smoothly. Breakfast, chores, the Five Tibetans, meditation, reading, and I got to attend my first "Group." Group is the meeting held every morning in the POD, led by the mentors and Head Counselor. Head Counselor is a psychologist who is the POD's head counselor. It is a time to review the rules, read an edited version of the Albuquerque newspaper, and discuss different topics like domestic violence and Post Traumatic Stress Disorder.

The 45-minute Group session was interesting to me. It allowed me to connect with other inmates in a safe environment. I could tell quickly which inmates were medicated, which were angry, which were bored. Of the thirty people in the POD, only eight or nine of them were willingly participating in the Group. The others were there because they had to be.

Upon the completion of Group, I reached the attorney's office (they accepted my collect call) and talked to his assistant. She said they were expecting my call. The attorney was in trial that morning and would be available after 2. I told her I would do my best to call later.

I took a shower, went to stand in the sun, and found myself joined by several other inmates, including angel number 1, The Monk. I learned The Monk had a Buddhist background and, like me with Christianity, had become disenchanted with the religion while clinging to the spirituality of it. He had once committed to a monastery, only to become shocked at the greed of its leaders. He was now sure that he wanted to spend the rest of his life in a monastery, if he could find the right one. Therefore, once he completed his debt to society, he was going to visit several monasteries for a month at a time until he found one he could commit to.

I felt safe with The Monk and we developed a fast friendship where we discussed religion, politics, and many other topics. He was a Buddhist angel that agreed with me before this life time to help me adjust to life in jail. I often watched him read on his bunk or walk the floor draped in his grey blanket and saw visions of him as a Tibetan monk in orange garb. I'm not sure how I would have gotten through this time without him and the Universe knew that.

He explained commissary to me. He provided me with a weekly schedule of activities and, as the POD's librarian, allowed me to check out extra library books. He expanded on meditation techniques. He gifted me a Tai Chi book. It was his first time in jail and my first extended time so we looked out for one another and gave each other companionship.

A Tai Chi instructor came to the POD at noon that day. However, by that time, I was back in my cell so I couldn't participate with the class. Again, I decided to make the best of the situation. My cell door had a glass window and there were two windows, one above the other, beside the door so I could observe the class and participate. I imitated the movements and listened through the door to the instruction. I didn't understand every word but it was a brief introduction to a new discipline that I had only heard about previously.

Later that afternoon, an inmate led a yoga class. Again, I participated by watching through the cell windows and listening through the door. I did the floor asana practices on my bunk and the standing ones on the floor.

By the time our afternoon lockdown was over, the entire facility was under lockdown. "Lockdown" means inmates must stay in our cells. There is no opportunity to go into the general population or move about freely. Normal lockdown times are form 8 pm to 7 am and again from 2 pm to 4 pm.

Lockdown for me was different, depending on the CO. Most COs would let me out of my cell for Group or, if not then, for lunch. The evening COs would let me out for 30 minutes most of the time. Some would let me out for dinner and allow me to stay out until 8. After the first couple of days, the daily COs would let me stay out for at least a couple of hours and often until 2 pm.

In instances where "something special" is taking place, the entire facility can be locked down for an extended period. This was the kind of lockdown I faced today. The phone call with the attorney would wait until Monday.

This lockdown was accompanied by a fire alarm that kept going off. It chirped in a patter of 3 on and one off and, at times, would sound for 5-10 minutes for no apparent reason. I spent the evening reading, doing Hindu squats, and listening to the alarm. Sleep came easily for me.

It didn't last.

A new inmate came in around 3:30 and was put beside me in Cell 8. I knew the time because the first thing he did was yell at the guard and ask "What time is it?" He sounded drunk or angry or both. He asked the CO for soap, a toothbrush, and anything else he could think of. Every sound reverberated throughout the POD and I wondered when he would go to sleep so I wouldn't have to listen to him. The answer came quickly enough.

Apparently, he was a drummer in his outside life and, after completing his conversation with the CO, he sat down at his desk and began to drum. He used the toilet, the sink, and the desk to create simple and complex rhythms. At first, the sound was annoying. Then, I remembered my decision about choices and decided to be grateful instead of complaining.

Since I couldn't sleep, I put on my critical ear and began to listen to it. Music was an intricate part of most of my life. I played in the band and sang in the choir while in high school. I had just enough ability to win a few awards, travel with select groups to Europe and through the United States, and be voted "most talented" in my small Virginia high school.

I spent four years at East Carolina University getting a degree in Music Education and subsequently taught private music lessons for ten years. In addition to my teaching experience, I played in numerous groups and often worked as a church musician. At the time, I didn't understand marketing well enough to make a living with music so I put it aside to pursue what I thought were more lucrative fields. I'm still an adequate "fake musician" and I know enough about music to be able to evaluate the skill level of the musicians.

As I consciously listened to The Drummer play, I realized he could play complex rhythms while keeping a steady tempo going underneath those rhythms. The average person can't do this. The fact that he was accomplishing this difficult task using a makeshift drum set was even more amazing. Even the most accomplished drummers from my past had to have everything set up just right if they were going to do what my new neighbor was doing. The sounds went from annoying to soothing. For the rest of the early morning, they woke me, put me to sleep, and woke me again.

His drumming continued through my early morning routine of breakfast, TFT, and cleaning my cell. His rhythms were joined by the facility faulty fire alarm, flushing toilets, POD telephone, and beeping sally port door and created a cacophony of sound that alternated between soothing and startling. I read my book and wondered when lockdown would end.

The answer was "not today." I finished reading Squeeze Play and with nothing else to do or read, I picked up the Bible The Preacher had given me during his visit. There was a project I had wanted to do for a while and since I couldn't do anything else, it seemed like a good time to do it.

I wanted to see if the words of Jesus taught the blood atonement for sins. This was important to me because if Jesus didn't teach the primary doctrine of the Christian faith, then it wasn't that important to him. If it wasn't that important to Jesus, then he saw the problem of sin differently from the way much of Christianity sees it today.

This may seem like a trivial issue. It is not. My first arrest taught me that judgment and punishment in our society can never be fair because of perspective. Right and wrong are opinions, loosely defined by the law, that give one person the "right" to control another. Once an individual perceives that someone else has done something wrong, a phone call can be made, an investigation can begin, and someone can be arrested.

Our first arrest was that way. We were having a drink with our own children, in our own house, and a visitor thought that was wrong. They reported us. Even though the NM law specifically says this is NOT illegal, we were arrested, had to pay bond, hire an attorney, and go through a CYFD[1] investigation. The perspective of the visitor said it was wrong. The perspective of the investigating officer said it was wrong. The law said it was right. We were arrested anyway.

The District Attorney wouldn't prosecute because the Sheriff's office wouldn't cooperate with the investigation so we were never indicted. Still, the emotional and mental trauma was significant. Who gave out more abuse that evening? Us, by having a drink with our kids, or the authorities, who ran through the house at 1:30 AM asking the kids how much they had to drink and arresting their parents?

---

[1] CYFD stands for Children, Youth, and Families Department. It is a State of New Mexico Agency.

The answer depends on one's perspective. This is troublesome because perspective determines reality and allows reality to become truth. In other words, one person's opinion can become truth and set off a chain of events that may kill millions of people in a 2000 year period.

Lest you think I exaggerate, we can look at one man, known as Paul. Paul wrote most of the New Testament and his writings are the basis for much Christian theology. This theology says man is sinful; therefore, man is guilty and must be punished by death. Punishment creates fear, especially when the potential punishment is death. This concept of death being punishment for sin has been used to justify numerous wars and other acts of atrocity for the past 2000 years.

What gave Paul the authority to establish Christian doctrine? There is no evidence he knew Jesus while Jesus was alive. Instead, Paul had several mystical experiences that stopped him from destroying Christians. As a result of his experiences, Paul changed from punishing Christians to punishing sinners.

I wanted to see if Paul's theology was Jesus' theology. When I previously practiced fundamental, evangelical Christianity, I accepted that the two theologies were one and I read the Bible with that filter. Now that I had been away from the Christian faith for several years, I wanted to read Jesus' words without that bias.

As I read Matthew, Mark, and Luke, I was struck by the similarities between the three books. I was reminded that many scholars believe that these books were taken from a common source often called the "Q" Gospel. I was also struck by the many contradictions, such as the explanation for why Jesus was called a Nazarene. I noticed the numerous healings and miracles performed by Jesus. I saw repeated teachings regarding growth, mercy, and love. Jesus never taught sin equals death and death must have a blood sacrifice for atonement. He made brief mention of his blood during the Passover meal commonly called "The Last Supper" The comment was slight and made without elaboration. I determined that if Jesus was attempting to teach the doctrine of blood sacrifice and atonement, he did a poor job of it.

As I read through John's gospel, I was impressed by the spiritual insight. When Jesus was asked about judgment, he responded by breaking laws and performing miracles. He blatantly performed acts of love and compassion while challenging the day's legal code. He addressed sin as an evil perpetuated by religious leaders while forgiving all others. He even went so far as to "reprove (disapprove) sin, righteousness, and judgment" and said, "You are gods" when the religious leaders sought to kill him because he claimed to be one with God. In other words, Jesus disapproved of the current ideology of sin, righteousness, and judgment. He didn't think it was necessary to teach or emphasize any of those topics.

By the time I finished the gospels, I was convinced that if the road to Salvation preached by today's Christian church was important, Jesus would have taught it. He didn't. In fact, it is a stretch to say Jesus even hinted at it. This isn't to say that it isn't helpful for certain people at certain times in life. However, to say it is Jesus' teaching is a statement that lacks credibility or evidence.

As I finished reading the four gospels, I heard the sounds of a roaring crow, sneakers on hardwood, blowing of whistles. The POD TV had been turned to a basketball game. I peered through my window and immediately recognized Cameron Indoor stadium, home of the Duke Blue Devils. I wondered how long the TV had been on. I had lost myself in the sounds of The Drummer, my reading, my thoughts about Jesus' teachings.

I love watching Duke play basketball. Coach Mike Krzyzewski's team always plays with intensity, no matter what the score. It is an approach that makes his team fun to watch, even if it sometimes drains them by the end of the season. I took a break from my reading to watch the game and realized I had missed most of it. They finished off an out-manned St. Louis team and I debated what to do next.

I remembered that my choices were limited. I could read. I could watch the Army-Navy football game that was now on TV. I could workout. I could meditate. I decided to do it all. I continued reading the New Testament and took breaks to do Hindu squats, check on the game score, do a yoga pose or two, and meditate on what I was reading.

As I read the book of Acts, I noticed how those who think differently are often locked up by authorities. The obvious comparisons to my situation allowed me to consider that incarceration was necessary for me to communicate clearly the ideas I use when I coach and teach seminars. I remembered Jesus' instructions to his disciples when they were reproached because of his teachings. He told them not to consider what they would say because it would be given them. He taught them not to "give thought for tomorrow." This is consistent with "New Age" and Buddhist teachings to stay in the moment.

I didn't want to presume that I was some great spiritual guru. However, I had to consider the history of great thinkers who were imprisoned for their ideology. Nelson Mandela, Gandhi, Martin Luther King, Jr., and many others were imprisoned because they stood for love, compassion, and human rights. Was my situation similar? I suppose the reader will have to decide based on this writing.

Our charges stem from a time when our family mutually decided to live a naked lifestyle. This was a decision we made with careful consideration. It all started in the summer of 2006. We have friends who owned a section of the Pecos River that winds through a box canyon. We spent several weekends there that summer. The privacy and seclusion attracted us just as it attracted explorers in the 1600s and United States Presidents in the 1900s.

During one visit, I noticed that some of my family was skinny dipping in the "fishing hole," one of the few areas on the property deep enough for swimming. They laughed at me and invited me to join them but I thought the water, fed by summer snowmelt, was too cold. During a subsequent visit, I thought I might actually skinny dip. However, the water was too low to go swimming.

Since I couldn't truly skinny dip, I decided to do something else I'd never done before, wade through the water sans clothes. I was in a private area of the river but I still felt vulnerable. My motivation was simply to have a new experience. I didn't know I would discover something deeper.

I grew up in a conservative, religious environment. My family, my church, my school, and my community had similar beliefs. Those beliefs covered many topics. One of those topics was nudity. The message to me was very clear. "Nudity is wrong."

There were only three exceptions:

1. A doctor can see a nude person because that's his job.
2. A married couple can see each other nude.
3. A baby can be seen nude because that's the only way to change its diaper.

High school and college were more of the same. Classes taught me the inappropriateness of nudity. If a liberal professor opened the door to new ideas on the topic, my classmates and I quickly slammed it shut.

When I married The Wife, we discussed nudity. We decided we were OK with it around each other but we didn't want to be nude around our kids. When our children were born, we used exception number 3 to change their diapers. However, once our children were old enough, we stressed the importance of clothing to cover the body. We taught them what we were taught.

In spite of these teachings to the contrary, I found myself deciding to take a nude walk down the Pecos River. This action certainly did not fit within any of the three exceptions.

As I enjoyed the water and the scenery, something significant happened deep within me. I experienced nature without barriers. I sensed new freedom. I felt a greater awareness of love deep within me. I felt it but I couldn't explain it. I decide to walk nude again the next day and see if I can figure it out.

Between my walks in the river, I read a book by Deepak Chopra. The title of the book was *The Spontaneous Fulfillment of Desire – Harnessing the Infinite Power of Coincidence.* In it, he observes that a divine force connects the universe. It is apparent in everything – especially nature. He uses the examples of birds in flocks and fish in schools. Here are his words.

> *They all seem to be moving in formation. When they change direction, they all execute the same motions synchronistically.*
>
> *A single school of fish can include hundreds of individuals, yet each fish moves in harmony with every other fish without an obvious leader. They change direction in an instant, all fish altering their course at the exact same moment, and they do it perfectly. You never see fish bumping into each other as they swim. They look like a single organism as if some unspoken command was issued that they all obeyed at once. How is that happening? There is not enough time for any exchange of information, so any correlation of activity among the fish must be happening non-locally.*
>
> *The instantaneous communication we commonly see in schools of fish comes from the spiritual level, the organizing nonlocal intelligence in the virtual domain. The result is synchronicity, beings that are totally in tune with their environment and with each other, dancing to the rhythm of the cosmos.*

The next day, as I again walked nude through the Pecos River, I noticed pools full of trout fingerlings. Every time I approached a pool, I saw examples of how the fish moved as a single organism. The trout moved in perfect sync with one another in response to my presence. There was no leader, no command given, just a perfect alignment of intent and connection.

This didn't surprise me. I'd seen it many times before. Fish do it. Birds do it. It is evident in many examples of nature. However, I had never considered those movements as evidence of a divine source orchestrating the events. I reasoned that if it is true for birds and fish, it must be true for the events in my life too.

Over the next several weeks, I thought about my experience. I shared it with my friends. Responses ranged from surprise to horror. I heard questions like, "Weren't you afraid someone would see you?", "Did you get sunburned?", and "Who went with you?" No one provided insight to my spiritual feelings. My friends were too shocked about my "outrageous action" to consider the deeper significance.

I thought more about my experience. I used it as a focus for my meditation. My reading took me through a passage in Volume 2 of *Conversation with God* written by Neale Donald Walsch. The topic was visibility. The author talked with God about visibility in relationships, visibility in business, and visibility in government.

This wasn't the type of visibility where we promote ourselves through advertising, smooth talk and public service announcements. It was the type where everything we do is visible to others. They see us. They see our motives. They see who we really are. There are no secrets.

As I read the book's dialogue, I realized the ramifications of visibility are tremendous. Friends learn to trust us. Customers know our costs and recognize the fairness in our pricing. Governments negotiate in good faith. There are no secrets.

As the dialogue continued, the topic evolved from visibility to nakedness. God and Mr. Walsch assumed that lovers are comfortable being physically naked in front of each other but, what about emotional nakedness? Can married partners, lovers, and life partners experience emotional nakedness with one another?

Mr. Walsch, who had experienced several divorces, concluded that emotional nakedness was much more difficult than physical nakedness. God agreed and challenged him to be a catalyst to change the world. God literally dared Neale Donald Walsch to change the world through the concept of emotional nakedness.

I understood that challenge because, at that moment, I gained understanding of what I felt when I walked in the river. Physical nakedness is an object lesson for emotional nakedness. That's what I felt in the river. That's why I felt love. The removal of clothing barriers led to the removal of emotional barriers.

Our modern society teaches us to cover feelings. The common opinion is that it is OK to feel as long as that feeling isn't expressed in a way that makes others uncomfortable. We become afraid of what others think. It is such an ingrained part of our lifestyle that we take it for granted. This produces communication problems. We want other people to understand us but we don't give them enough information to understand us. Businesses, families, and friendships suffer damage because of assumptions, cover-ups, lack of communication, and lies.

On the other hand, emotional nakedness means there are no secrets. We share our feelings. We talk about our hurts. We work through situations with no hidden agendas. The flow of conversations and feelings is refreshing and pure, just like the cold water rushing over my legs on a summer day.

This truth resonated within me. I realized that human beings mutate our spiritual abilities by covering our feelings, our thoughts, and our bodies. I wondered if the simple uncovering of my body while visiting the river began turning me from a "mutant" into a human again.

I shared this information with my family and we discussed nudity. The discussion was simple. Everyone had the opportunity to talk about his or her feelings on the subject. Some stated they were ready to participate immediately. Others wanted to participate but they needed time to redo their programming. (Remember, we had taught them the importance of clothing when they were younger.) Everyone agreed that they didn't mind other people's nudity.

We discussed nude etiquette (always sit on a towel). We agreed to communicate clearly regarding visitors so there were no surprises. We decided to see what would happen because of our new understandings. Initially, there wasn't much nudity practiced outside of the hot tub and the privacy of our own bedrooms. However, as time went by, we each became more comfortable with wearing less clothing.

Then, the remarkable started to happen.

We discovered that the ability to remove clothing made it easier to remove the barriers in other parts of our lives too. Our children began to talk to us about a long-standing problem with their home schooling. An older child talked about a new experience he had previously been unwilling to share. New business opportunities fell into our laps.

This is not to say that we were naked all the time. In fact, with all that was going on in our lives, it was usually more convenient to wear clothing. We often had guests in our home and, some stayed with us for an extended period. One woman, House Guest, moved into our guest room for almost nine months. Moving her into our home was a purely intuitive act that didn't really make sense at the time. She stayed with us from January through September and she wasn't comfortable with nudity so we respected her wishes and didn't practice it. When she moved out, she told us we had saved her life. She had intended to move in, kill herself, and leave her stuff with us. However, when she saw it was possible to live life with love, she sought healing, received it, and changed her mind.

Once House Guest moved out, we chatted about going back to some nudity in the household. However, with the cooler weather it wasn't practical. More importantly, we were out of practice and the naked communication wasn't happening.

Son One was dealing with his relationship with Son One's Partner. She would talk to him and not talk with us. That meant he wasn't talking to us about it unless we initiated the conversation. Daughter Three had started a relationship with a boyfriend who was an extremely conservative Christian and she wanted to explore conservative Christianity herself. Therefore, she wasn't open in her communication either. I wasn't opposed to her exploring Christianity as long as she was consistent in living Christian principles. However, I knew that people, especially teenagers, often hide within some new philosophy because it is different and makes their new religion "being different to be different" instead of honestly exploring the philosophy.

I always challenged our children to think about the "whys" of their actions so they could practice integrity. Their belief system didn't have to be my belief system. I just wanted them to know what they believed and to live their lives consistent with that belief.

Of course, since different people were going in different ways, it was going to take a while for us to get to where we were after our experience in the Pecos River. Those were wonderful times. We practiced open (naked) communication, learned that nudity was NOT about sex and often hugged one another as a way of saying "hello" or "goodbye." We saw our children grow in love and understanding as we were reminded daily of the importance of open communication in building community and extended family. We could practice a naked lifestyle in a safe environment without worrying about accusations of sexual abuse and without worries of sexual activity between family members.

I should stop here and say that when I use the word "sexual" in the above paragraph, I'm referring to actions that lead to orgasm. In other words, conscious, purposeful actions along with communication that says, "I want to be your sexual partner." We taught our children that sex should always be consensual, that sex isn't something you do to someone else, and it isn't something someone else does to you. It is conscious and purposeful, not something you fall into in a moment of passion.

In addition, we taught that sexual passion or sexual energy doesn't have to be used to complete a sex act. In fact, this energy can easily be used to cook a meal, wash a car, or close a sale. The reason is simple. Sexual energy is just energy. Each person decides how he or she will use it.

Of course, we talked about using protection and we kept a supply of condoms on hand. We explained that it was OK and even necessary to talk with potential partners about birth control, sterilization, and STDs. I'm sure the kids were sometimes uncomfortable with the conversations because the topic was new to them and society tends not to talk about it. However, I was determined they have all the information they needed to make the decisions they needed to make.

I watched Son One and Son One's Partner go through their relationship using these techniques. They talked about having a baby. They decided to have a baby and Son One's Partner is now pregnant. Her personality quirks became an issue and we've experienced challenges as a result. However, they did exactly what we had taught them in regards to the sexual part of their relationship. We were still working on the other parts.

On November 17, during our family meeting, it was Son Two's turn to lead the discussion and he made an impassioned plea for us to move back to nakedness, especially in regards to communication. I was proud of him. It was the first time any of our kids had spoken with that type of energy about any subject. In most cases, they listened to my ideas, asked questions, and we came to an agreement on the next step with their input. I had recently backed out of the leadership of our daily meetings.

43

I purposely became the facilitator and encouraged each person to lead the meeting once every couple of weeks.

When Son Two completed his request, I asked for a response from each person. Daughter Three said, "No, thank you, you may do so but I don't want to participate." The Wife, Son One, Son Three, and Daughter Two agreed with Son Two. Daughter Four and Son Four said they wanted to think about it. We decided if everyone wasn't ready to move forward that we needed to wait to do so. We also decided to keep the topic alive so we could deal with it.

For the past several years, this was typical of how we ran our family. We brought up a topic and debated it, looking for something insightful to discuss or share. In many cases, we just compiled information and didn't act. In other cases, we agreed to meditate on an issue and come back to the Group with ideas. There were ample opportunities to do this. The family members who lived at the house held a meeting each Monday through Friday at 6 AM and on Saturday morning at 7 unless we needed to change the time. The extended family met weekly to review school and financial goals and discuss long term goals. In addition, because extended family members were there, we discussed controversial subjects such as government conspiracy theories and alternative lifestyles.

It was in one of these meetings where we all agreed to create a safe environment for safely exploring a naked lifestyle several years ago. Each person proceeded at his or her own pace and if someone struggled with nudity, we asked questions. We wanted to see if it was possible for this to work and if someone wasn't participating, we wanted to know why it wasn't working for them. As I said earlier, our goal was to live in integrity. Therefore, if someone agreed to do something, we held them accountable to doing it unless they wanted to change the agreement. Changing the agreement was permissible provided the individual initiating the change communicated with everyone involved. Daughter Three started this process during that morning meeting but we weren't allowed to finish it.

Instead of taking the time to talk with us about this, she complained to her boyfriend. Her boyfriend told his dad, who talked with his pastor, an ex-cop. Juvenile laws being what they are, they felt obligated to call CYFD. Therefore, on the night of November 17, Bernalillo County Sheriff Office (BCSO) deputies knocked at our door to talk to me about that phone call. After a half hour conversation, they were satisfied with my explanation and they let us go back to bed.

Then, on November 18, BCSO returned, led by a Detective, and accompanied by a CYFD representative. They literally raided our house and took Daughter Three, Daughter Four, and Son Four to live with The Wife's parents while they began an investigation. We were crushed. However, my experience more than twenty years ago as a juvenile corrections officer told me there was nothing I could do about it until the investigation was complete.

The family members still in our house decided the best thing we could do was to support one another and dig into our business activity with a renewed energy so we could fill the gaps left by the missing children.

Besides my accounting and coaching work, our family builds websites and does marketing. We also run a mobile detailing company. We have a mobile cleaning unit, a mobile appearance repair unit, and a unit at the local airport. Son Four had been helping Son Three at the airport while Daughter Three worked with Son One on the mobile cleaning unit. Son Two ran the repair unit and he and Daughter Two provided days off for each person so they could work on school. Daughter Four and the person who had the day off watched Daughter One's kids so she could work for me.

With the three younger kids removed from the house, seven people were doing the work of ten. Of course, now that The Wife and I were in jail, five people were doing the work of ten while trying to deal with the emotional impact of our situation.

As far as I can tell, the younger three children were interviewed by CYFD on December 2 and asked about the time when we lived a naked lifestyle. Then, based on that conversation, a BCSO detective scheduled interviews for The Wife and me on December 8. We were told the purpose of the interviews was to hear our side of the story so we could move towards reuniting our family. Instead, the purpose was to charge us with a felony for every time we hugged a child.

One of our goals had been to learn to live a naked life in the same way we would a clothed life, without any hang-ups about being nude. Now, we were suspected child abusers for doing that.

As I read the book of Acts and saw that the Apostles were imprisoned for sharing a message of love, I had to look at my situation and make comparisons. I was in jail not because I had hurt or abused someone. I was in jail because I dared to tear down the barriers of love and communication. Was it worth it? I didn't know the answer to that yet, but I reasoned that if our kids learned the value of open communication through this process, it could be.

My meditation time today was interrupted by things I needed to say to The Wife and kids. This happened so many times that I knew I must do something about it. I didn't have pen and paper so I couldn't write down those things. After thinking about this for a while, I remembered some writings, including Richard Bach's, where people managed to astral travel to other places. They would visit other people and communicate telepathically. I had read this technique was effective, even when the other person wasn't "tuned in."

I decided to try this before I went to sleep that evening by visiting each person in my family. I lay on my back, put my hands over my chest, closed my eyes, and imagined myself flying up into the sky and then going to visit every member of my family including the grandkids and The Chihuahua, my Daughter One's pet dog. Each person engaged me in conversation and it was a wonderful experience for me. None of them were conscious of me except possibly my granddaughter Grandchild Two (more about that below) and The Chihuahua. However, I discovered later that at least two of them benefitted from the communication.

Daughter One told me that for several days after the arrest, 20 year-old Son Three looked like a 35 year-old man. Then, he suddenly looked normal again. I suspected my subconscious conversation with him was the key to his recovery.

During my subconscious conversation with Son One, I identified with the emotion he was feeling and realized he needed to move to Illinois to be with Son One's Partner. I'm still certain they will struggle, but that's OK and if they fall on their faces, we'll be able to help them. A couple nights later, he announced to the family that he was moving to Illinois.

My conversation with Grandchild Two was amazing. Just a few days before my arrest, I had attempted to communicate with her telepathically when she woke up from a nap. As soon as I started to do so, she turned her head towards, me, smiled, and talked back to me telepathically. We did this off and on for the rest of the day. I was amazed when I learned that other people could experience this and completely thrilled that I could too.

I had been prompted to try this by a book called *The Children of Now*. The premise of this book is that certain children born into this generation have a special gift and are a special gift to the world. They are here to communicate love to all.

I suspected Grandchild Two was one of these children. She had already been singled out through a phone conversation The Wife had with a friend of a friend that The Wife had never met. This woman didn't know The Wife had any grandkids; however, she told her the new baby girl in her family would speak to her and teach her things so be sure to listen to her.

I subconsciously chatted with Grandchild Two about my situation and she said she knew and she understood. She smiled as she told me to be strong and rejoice in what would come from this.

With my conversations complete, I went to sleep in spite of The Drummer and the unpredictable fire alarm.

Sunday, December 12, 2010

Sleeping in my cell at MDC was a challenge for the first few nights. I had two blankets and a three inch thick mattress that was about six feet long and 30 inches wide. I used one blanket as a pillow and the other for warmth. Sleeping on my back caused my hips to hurt and sleeping on my side caused my shoulder to go to sleep. I kept experimenting with different angles and finally discovered that if I pulled the mattress up on the end of the bunk, I had a perfect setting for sleeping on my back or on my side. I learned that by exercising hard each day and fatiguing myself, I slept well every night and the noises didn't bother me. I was grateful for the rest.

I completed my morning routine and, since the lockdown continued, I read the next book of the New Testament. It had some surprises for me.

The book of Romans is used by many Christian churches and organizations as the basis for what they call the "Roman Road to Salvation." I hadn't thought about this "road" for many years; however, when I read those verses, I was reminded of it. I wondered why they used these select verses to state their case. Were they clarifying something already in scripture or were they making up something that wasn't there? By the time I got to chapter 11, I knew the answer. The author had come to the same conclusion I had in my almost fifty years of studying spirituality: God has given atonement (at-one-ment) to all people and it has nothing to do with a blood sacrifice. It has everything to do with living within the Christ Spirit.

I read through the other letters of the New Testament and experienced the confusion of the authors as they attempted to deal with Church issues and various details of the law. I wondered how Paul and the other writers felt about their letters becoming "Holy Writ" and I decided to ask them that night by talking to them using the same technique I used when talking to my family last night.

My morning reading was interrupted by the CO calling my name on the intercom. He told me I had a visit. Visitation at MDC takes place on a video phone. I had never used one before. I went and sat on the stool in the POD's visitation room and waited. Finally, Son Two showed up on the screen. He cried when he heard my voice and I immediately told him I was doing well and that he didn't need to worry about me.

We talked about business and the family. I told him about my "trip" to see everyone last night, about working out, and my attitude to make this a spiritual retreat. He told me about what was going on with the family and business. Then, he told me about the support system that was developing. He said that people wanted to send the family money and that College Friend was sending $5000. Did I hear him correctly? People were sending us money and one person had already put a check in the mail for five grand? We cried with joy. It was the first time I had cried since the arrest. He told me he put $30 into my commissary account. That meant I could purchase phone cards, tablets, and pens.

I finished the visit and went back into my room to finish my cry. The Drummer continued to play and I danced. I had to dance. The joy in my heart had gone to my feet. The Drummer played and I danced.

I danced and cried as I thought of College Friend's gift. I met College Friend in the fall of 1979. I was a freshman music major at East Carolina University and she, an upperclassman nursing major, was taking marching band because it was fun. She walked across the field, came up to me, and introduced herself. We became fast friends but never dated. She was the highlight of my early college experience. She showed me around campus, introduced me to several student groups, and even took me home with her to Florida for spring break.

After graduation, we maintained minimal contact until a few years ago when her work brought her to Albuquerque. She came to our home for Sunday dinner and, after more than 25 years, our friendship continued without missing a beat. The following spring, Daughter Three and I visited College Friend's Georgia home on the way back from a trip to Virginia to help my parents move into their apartment. It was during that visit that College Friend inspired me to start my coaching business and she agreed to become my first client. For the third time in my life, here she was again, showing up in a powerfully tangible way at a vital time.

As I finished my dance, I floated out into the general population where people were complaining about The Drummer. Lockdown was over but everyone was grumpy about the lack of sleep they'd gotten thanks to The Drummer. This was interesting to me because my room was beside his and I'd slept great. My decision not to complain about what I couldn't control was yielding benefits.

51

I thought to myself, "When life sends you lemons, make lemonade and when life sends you a Drummer, dance." No one seemed interested in being cheered up so I floated outside to walk under the New Mexico blue sky and to enjoy the sunshine.

During my walk, I heard a crow's "caw, caw, caw." Crows have always been around me and I suddenly felt a connection to this common bird as if it was somehow there to tell me it all would be OK. I stopped and looked up through the fence into the sky and longed for the crow to fly overhead so I could see it. It didn't.

I continued my dance walk around the outside area. Suddenly, much louder, I heard "caw, caw, caw." I looked up and a crow flew over the little slice of sky that I could see. The tears flowed freely down my cheeks as I danced and twirled in the sunlight. (Amazingly, I saw a crow almost every day while I was in MDC. It was the only live plant or animal I saw while here and it brought me great hope and courage every time I saw it.)

Since it was Sunday, I was able to sit with The Monk and watch football until our 2:00 lockdown. We traded stories, enjoyed the game, and it felt like old times. I suspected I knew The Monk from another place and time.

The rest of the day was uneventful. I was moved from Cell 9 to Cell 7 so they could admit a guy in cuffs. Cell 7 had a solid door. Cell 9's door had a chuck door so they could put a new inmate into the cell handcuffed and then open the chuck door to remove the cuffs. Cell 7 was identical to Cell 9 and, since The Drummer was in Cell 8, I was still beside him. He had now played drums for almost 48 hours. This confirmed my earlier guess that he was angry or under the influence of a "foreign substance" or both since he was able to play for that length of time.

I finished my day by talking to the New Testament writers about their contributions. I chatted with John, Peter, Paul, Timothy, and James. My initial intent was to talk with one at a time. However, when the conversation started, they all showed up at once. I was reminded of the virtual mastermind meetings that Napoleon Hill writes about in *Think and Grow Rich*. Mr. Hill would hold meetings in his imagination with great minds of the past. He said the meetings were always insightful and that the individuals often behaved in ways that surprised him.

My experience was similar. When I started asking questions, the writers were embarrassed that their writings had become "God's Word." They said their writings were attempts to clarify their own thoughts about certain topics and if they had been attempting to establish church doctrine, they would have done so in a systematic method. They pointed out that the numerous greetings at the end of some books were certainly not the "inspired word of God." They were just "saying hi" to their friends. They felt that many people gave the written word too much weight over the "living word" that is available through prayer.

The writer of Romans, Paul, agreed to stay after everyone else left and talk to me about that book. He said it wasn't until he finished the letter to the Romans that he understood the sin problem. Initially, he wanted to have an excuse to punish those who didn't agree with him and he thought sin was a way to do that. His early religious training had given him that motivation. He said that while writing the letter to the Romans, he realized that if the Christ Spirit lived within someone for salvation, it also kept that person from sinning. He reasoned that if the Christ Spirit couldn't keep someone from sinning, it couldn't bring salvation. He had a difficult time accepting that concept until he realized he was defining sin as breaking man's law, including any law written by man that was called "God's law." He said he realized that every law could and would be broken by someone. This wasn't because mankind was evil. It was because mankind was creative and every system of law had contradictions within it that made it impossible to follow.

He said he recognized that nothing, not even sin, could separate a person from God because God is everywhere. He realized that everyone would be "reunited" with God and that he was hesitant even to use that word because a person's sense of separation from God is an illusion. Of course, if a person thinks he is separated from God that will be his perceived reality, even if it isn't true. He said that people who think they are separated from God use punishment to control other people. In other words, it is a belief that sin exists, not the act of sin that causes a person to believe he is separated from God.

He said he only came to clarity on that while he was writing the book to the Romans so anything he wrote prior to that time contained the influence of his earlier religious teaching rather than the teachings of Jesus.

We talked about other issues too but those were the most important ones. He asked me to be sure I addressed the "sin topic" in my book, even if I suspected people wouldn't be receptive to the message. He expressed sorrow that his words had been used to oppress people for the past two thousand years and he thanked me for my courage.

After he left, I knew that I had to write this book. The idea first came to me just minutes after my arrest. The inspiration for the topics flooded my mind when I meditated or went to sleep. I have read about other writers who said they wouldn't write for months or years and then, suddenly, they had to write. My experience was that entire paragraphs would flow into my memory. This concerned me during my first week in jail because I had no way to write them down. I was afraid I'd forget them and desperately wanted to write but I had no way to do so. I finally rested in the knowledge that if they flowed once, they'd flow again. I was never disappointed. They always showed up again when I picked up my pen.

Monday, December 13, 2010

I began today with my routine of breakfast, meditation, chores, exercise, and reading. The Drummer continued to play throughout the night and I was further amazed at his stamina. With the reading of the New Testament finished, I started on the Old Testament. I read though Genesis and learned a great deal from the story of Joseph.

Joseph was sold by his brothers as a slave into Egypt because of his dreams. His ability to interpret dreams made him a leader in the country until he was falsely accused of sexual misconduct. After several years, his skills were made known again and he once again became a leader. This time, it was during a severe famine in the land. His foresight and wisdom saved the country and eventually brought citizens of neighboring areas to Egypt for food. When Joseph's family arrived, he staged a dramatic series of events and was reunited with his entire family.

I felt Joseph's emotions as he reunited with his family. I also recognized that my current situation is being orchestrated by God to prepare our family for an emotional reconciliation in the future. I rested content that the suffering of this present time was nothing compared to the glory that will be revealed in us.

I was let out of my cell mid-morning and called the attorney's office. I was told he was planning to visit me so I rested on that. I took a shower, put myself on the "shaver list," and chatted with The Monk while waiting for my turn with the electric razor.

I was pleasantly surprised at the shower and showering situation at MDC. The shower area had six stations, three tall ones and three short ones. There was no privacy, except for a short wall between the showering areas and the general area. I chuckled to myself about this being the opportunity for me to "live a naked life" in jail and didn't worry about who was looking. Again, I knew I couldn't control the situation so why worry about it?

The water was controlled by a push button that provided eleven seconds of perfectly heated water through a high spray nozzle. At the end of those eleven seconds, the water turned off and I'd have to punch the button again. My daily shower was several minutes of luxury that I cherished. I took my time, enjoying each sensation of the water and often envisioned the water washing my emotional baggage down the drain.

The electric razor was available to use on Monday, Wednesday, and Friday. Surprisingly, it was a top-of-the-line Norelco. The mentor in charge of the razor made sure it was sanitized between each use.

The Monk was in charge of the razor today and I chatted with him while inmates were using the razor. During our conversation, I noticed a tall attractive woman enter the POD. She seemed familiar to me but I couldn't place her. She walked up to the COs desk and said "Matthew Cox." I moved in her direction to introduce myself and realized who she was. It was My Attorney.

After my first arrest, I interviewed several attorneys. The first didn't want my case and recommended other attorneys, including My Attorney and her associate. The second was a young, sharp female that I liked tremendously. The third was My Attorney's associate. While waiting in jail during my first arrest, I had a vision of my phone ringing and a female attorney saying, "Hello, I've heard about your case and I want to be your attorney." Since this hadn't happened yet, I figured I'd have to make the decision based on the interviews.

On the way home from those interviews, I called The Wife to discuss them. I was inclined to go with attorney number two and was about to tell The Wife that when another call beeped on my phone. I took the call and said, "This is Matt." The voice on the other end said, "Hi Matt, I've heard about your case and I want to be your attorney." I listened politely a she explained her credentials but I already knew she was My Attorney. She told me she shared an office with her associate and encouraged me to hire her because her associate would be less expensive. In addition, she promised she would support her associate each step of the way.

Now, here she was, unsolicited by me, showing up to talk about my case. We sat down at a table and quickly went through the details. She explained that the state had ten days to indict me and that, if they didn't, I could get out the following day. She asked me if I could stand being in here that long. I told her I had already thought through that and I would be OK doing that.

She asked me about The Wife and I told her that it made sense for her too, but she'd need to talk to her. I told her about the other attorney's planned visit and let her know I'd be in touch with her the next day to retain her. She left to go visit The Wife and suddenly a floodgate of visitors opened for me.

A CYFD representative came by to update me on the custody of Daughter Three, Daughter Four, and Son Four. She told me they were OK at The Father-in-Law's and discussed other possible arrangements. We decided to wait through the indictment phase to make a change.

A representative from the Public Defender's Office came by and offered to take my case for $15,000. I told her "Thanks, but no thanks."

While talking with her, I noticed a medical staff member come into the POD with two rovers. Rovers were COs in training. They provided relief for the COs, performed suicide watch, and served as escorts to inmates going to court and medical. They opened Cell 8 and told The Drummer to get on his bunk and lay on his stomach. He did so and they gave him a shot in the arm. About thirty minutes later, his drumming ended for the first time in sixty hours.

My Attorney came by again and told me The Wife wasn't doing well. She felt mistreated and needed a change. As we stood discussing her, PAC 2 Psychiatrist walked through and we approached her with two requests. The first request was not to move me from my current POD. PAC 2 Psychiatrist had told me earlier they might need to move me. I wanted her to know I felt safe in the current situation and I thought telling her in front of My Attorney was a good idea. We also asked her to look into The Wife's situation and make sure she had access to shower and reading material.

My Attorney left and, within minutes, the other attorney showed up and we talked in private for an hour. We discussed my case and I could tell he was excited about the possibilities. We clicked and I debated whether to use him. I asked him about working with My Attorney in the event that The Wife and I needed different attorneys. He said he had in the past but he wouldn't again. I told him I'd be in touch and made no commitment to retain him.

By the time he left, it was time for lockdown and I had my attorney plan. I would call My Attorney the next day and get her promised update on the indictment. She would call the older kids, get a blank check from them, and bring it to me so I could retain her. Based on our conversation, she hoped to visit me again Wednesday morning, but it could be as late as Friday.

I turned back to the Bible for my afternoon reading. I finished Genesis and went into Exodus until I got to the Old Testament laws. I recoiled in horror at the atrocities the Bible blamed on God and I was astounded at the blood and destruction built into that religious system. I put the Bible down in disgust and paced my cell. This book was the source of so much rich teaching. However, it was also full of many destructive ideas and stories. It misrepresented God and provided excuses and justification for wars, murder, and taking plunder in God's name. For more than 35 years, I considered the Bible the divinely inspired word of God and I read it daily. When I moved away from my childhood Christianity, I took a vacation from the Bible so I would have time to read and study other material. I had recently felt a pull to go back and read the Bible again.

Now that I was reading it, I knew that if the Bible was the complete Word of God, that God had deep mental health issues and suffered a case of massive confusion. I believed God was love, life, and peace. God was not schizophrenic, angry, and vengeful. God was not fear, hate, judgment, and punishment. God was exploration, experimentation, and correction, gentle correction. God's correction wasn't based on a moral sense of right and wrong. But on a sense of efficiency based on what works and what doesn't work.

God is abundant and has provided everything we need at every time. God is needless in that God has no needs for us to obey a set of laws; therefore, it is not possible to offend God. God is eternal and therefore we are eternal, moving into and out of life over and over again. Death is not to be feared. In fact, nothing is to be feared because God is good all the time.

I remembered the joy and comfort I received from reading sections of the Bible the previous couple of days and I was grateful for God's voice in those sections. As my disgust with the Old Testament waned, I recognized that perhaps God allowed these sections to survive for thousands of years because God wanted to show what happens when religion tries to force its will on other people by calling it "God's will." The resulting manipulation, control, and bondage cause wars and destruction. God knew mankind would eventually recognize what works and what doesn't work by seeing that violence, even violence perpetuated for "moral reasons" was still violence, and the only way to achieve peace was to practice peaceful actions.

I saw only one way to go from confusion to clarity, bondage to freedom, hate to love, and war to peace. That is through the practice of clarity, freedom, love, and peace. I was grateful for this insight and saw it as a cornerstone for a new idea that had been forming in my mind for several months called The Peace of Mind Training Institute.

The Peace of Mind Training Institute (POMTI) was quickly coming to life as a powerful resource for those searching for Peace of Mind. In my transition from Christianity to my current belief system, I had to write a book to gain clarity. The book was *Living the Southwest Lifestyle; How to Have and Maintain Peace of Mind*. I originally intended to use "Living the Southwest Lifestyle" to teach Peace of Mind. However, the name became a point of confusion for people so we decided to change the name to Peace of Mind Training Institute. We even changed the name of our most y dormant 501(c)3 organization so we could be tax-exempt.

I knew that my current experience was deepening the Peace of Mind message and I knew the time I was taking to read the Bible was important for me. In fact, I was now 100% certain I could support the Peace of Mind message with the Bible in the same way any other theology was supported through proof-texting and preconceived biases. I still felt a pull to take my message to the Christian church and I often wondered how that would happen.

I craved new reading material and I knew that I would have the opportunity to get that after lockdown. We were allowed to go to "the library" on Monday, Wednesday, and Friday and I had heard this POD had a good library. Since there was still an hour left on lockdown, I decided to quit reading the Old Testament horror sections and read the book of Daniel. I figured that if reading about one dreamer (Joseph) had encouraged me, reading about another one was a good idea too.

The first chapter of Daniel brought me face to face with dietary decisions. Daniel and his buddies asked permission to skip the king's rich food and eat "pulse and water" instead. I think this means he was a vegetarian. I chuckled at the idea of trying to eat that way in MDC.

We received three meals a day between 3:30 am and 5 pm. I suspected they spread out the meals so far because the food was so bad and a person will eat almost anything when really hungry. Every meal, breakfast, lunch, and dinner came with two pieces of white bread. Breakfast had milk, some version of instant oatmeal, and cheap protein like powdered eggs or bologna. Lunch was always the bread with a slice of processed meat and a slice of processed cheese. We received canned fruit or pudding, a bag of corn chips and three cookies. Dinner was sometimes real food, but not always. It was the highlight of the day and included processed meat cooked in a variety of ways. It was usually served with noodles or pasta, an overcooked vegetable and a desert of tasteless cake or pudding.

I usually had to eat breakfast and dinner in my room. I often ate lunch in the commons area. As soon as any meal was served, the negotiating would begin. Cries of "chips for cookies," "sandwich for pudding," would echo off the walls. Trades would take place and everyone would eat. I often gave away my bread, but never traded. I ate the best most nutritious items on the tray and always made sure I finished anything raw, live, or containing fiber. By doing that, exercising, and drinking lots of water, I managed to keep my digestive system working throughout most of my stay.

I thought a while about Daniel's diet and was reminded that on the morning of our arrest, our family had decided to purchase a Vita Mix juicer and make super-food smoothies for our breakfast. The Wife and I were going to look at them at Costco after our interview. Of course, that never happened. After eating jail food, I suspected these unique smoothies would taste pretty good but I didn't know when I would get to try one.

I read the story of the three Hebrew boys and the fiery furnace and recognized God's plan during my time in jail. I read the dreams of the kings and Daniel and their interpretations and recognized that prophecies can be misunderstood or manipulated to mean many different things (more about that below). I read the story of Daniel in the Lion's Den and recognized that people are often locked up on the technicality of law even though love would say they've done nothing wrong.

The book of Daniel spoke to my heart and I was grateful. Of course, Daniel is filled with several prophecies and many Bible scholars think some of those have to do with end times. These scholars say the church is the kingdom mentioned in chapter 2 that will last forever. I realized this is not true because the church does not grow and consume other kingdoms. Love is the all-consuming "kingdom" and when I applied this understanding to all of the prophecies, they became clear and more encouraging to me.

I've studied prophecy for most of my life and, like most people, I'm fascinated with it. We all have a natural curiosity about the future. I have learned that all prophecy is accurate, even though not everything prophesied may take place. A prophecy is just one possible outcome for a series of events. It does not lock into place a prescribed series of events. If it did, this would limit the creative forces of the Universe, including each individual's creative ability.

For example, many people believe the Bible and other spiritual books predict a great destruction. While this is certainly possible, it is only one possibility. Other prophets are now coming forward who say something significant will happen in the next few years; however, the change doesn't have to be destructive. Instead, it can be completely productive and peaceful. If this happens, the only thing that will be destroyed is mankind's current fascination with controlling other people through the force of religious and government institutions.

More importantly, an obsession with future events takes one out of the moment. The process of being present with whatever a person is doing is the key to growth, well-being, peace, and happiness. I was learning this every day I stayed at MDC and I knew this skill would serve me well upon my release.

Speaking of release, when lockdown was over, I got to go to the library. I turned in *Squeeze Play* and looked anxiously on the shelf for something that would speak to me. My eyes were drawn to *The Blue Cord* by Laurel Duran. I remembered that Richard Bach wrote about the silver cord that connected his etheric body to his spiritual body during his astral travel. I hoped this book would provide more insight for me and give me some guidance as I experimented with this new practice.

I checked it out and, with a book in hand; I went back to my cell for a peaceful night of reading. Even though the drumming had stopped, the fire alarm was another issue. My cell insulated me from the painful decibel levels but I noticed those who lived in the common area were now wearing ear plugs they had fashioned out of toilet paper. There was no pattern to when the alarm would go off. Sometimes it would sound for 45 seconds and, on rare occasions; it would sound for as long as 45 minutes.

The Blue Cord was a fascinating story of a woman who had a near death experience when her neck was broken in an automobile accident. It described the love she felt as she was ushered into the presence of God. She then came back to this life and was able to use that feeling to help her through the challenges of her recovery. With her physical injury, she couldn't continue her work as a massage therapist. However, she learned to administer her new "love energy" and bring healing to those around her while she recovered physically.

During her experience in the hospital, she met two men facing a crisis of their own. One had almost killed the other during a robbery. The victim reached out to the attacker and through a miracle of love, the attacker became the victim's caregiver and the victim dropped the charges against the attacker. As they told her the story they explained that we "grow softly strong in the cracked places."

When I read that phrase, I broke and cried. The tears flowed unashamedly as I realized that every time we experience an injury, a crack, we have the opportunity to yell and scream while we resist and throw a temper tantrum or we can accept it, yield to it, and allow it to heal. This healing process in the body produces a scar and when complete, this scar tissue is stronger and thicker than the surrounding tissue. I knew this was me. I had been cracked by my arrest and my response was to accept it so I could grow strong. This time was to be my spiritual retreat, a place for me to prepare for the next part of my life. No computers, no cell phones, no radio, and limited TV; just me, my thoughts, and a book or two to inspire and guide me.

And I knew I had the title for my book.

Tuesday, December 14, 2010

The Drummer woke from his shot in the middle of the night and played his music once again. Again, his music alternated between waking me and lulling me to sleep.

After my morning routine, I finished reading *The Blue Cord* and struggled through a National Geographic Magazine.

I was allowed out of my cell to shower and participate in Group. I signed up for a haircut which didn't happen today. I worked out a lot, doing yoga, Hindu squats, and Hindu pushups. I had breezed through my reading material so I had to find something else to occupy my time. I decided to initiate conversations with the other inmates and observe behavior.

I watched as three rovers and a nurse went into The Drummer's cell to give him another shot. He didn't want more medicine so they forced him to strip and lay on his tummy. This time, they skipped his arm and gave the shot in his ass. I wondered why they medicate him at 11 in the morning knowing he would wake again at 10 or 11 that night and start drumming again. The Drummer knew we were watching and when the staff left the room, he responded by putting his butt cheeks against the glass and rubbing them against it.

With the POD excitement for the day completed, I decided to call My Attorney. I told her that I intended to retain her and she promised to see me in the next day or so.

During lunch, I watched as the food negotiations took on an unusual fervor. The medicated inmates usually avoided anything stressful. They either didn't have the motivation or, if they did have it, the drugs took it away. Today's chaos originated from The Vulture.

He claimed to be half black and half Indian. He had ebony skin and a mostly straight afro. The back half of the afro was long and woven into three inch long "dreadlocks." He sometimes combed them down. More often, they stood up straight making it look like he had a miniature headdress or bird's crown. He spent most of every meal looking for food that other inmates were not going to eat; a process I called "vulturing."

Today, he was being especially aggressive and making lots of enemies in the process. At the end of the meal, he stood by the place where we turned in trays and vultured everything left on anyone's tray.

I noticed that many of the inmates had a definite sense of lack. Several ate their lunch and took what wasn't wanted by others so they could eat all day. Others purchased snacks from the commissary so they could eat all day. Several of the inmates were obese and ate to cope with their issues. They worried about running out of food or not having enough and it showed in their behavior and elevated stress levels. The Vulture was the archetype for this.

By today, I finally felt like the media storm over our arrest had blown over. I had heard through the grapevine that we were all over the news, both TV and paper. I heard that some of our children and The Father-in-Law had made statements to the press. In addition, clients were calling to both offer support and request their accounting files. MDC does a pretty good job of removing these stories from the newspapers we read. However, the TV news is another story.

The second day I was in here, I introduced myself to another inmate and as I did, a third inmate said, "Did you say Matthew? You were just on the news." I said, "That probably wasn't me" and went straight to my cell. No one followed and no one threatened so that was a relief.

During dinner, I received my first piece of mail from someone who wasn't an attorney wanting my case. It was a packet of religious material from a former client. This client had a huge heart for jail inmates and wanted to save all of them. He used his limited funds from his business to support his jail and prison ministry. His business practices had already caused him to declare bankruptcy at least once and he was years behind on his state and federal taxes.

I reviewed the information and saw the underlying message of sin, punishment, and judgment. I could feel the anger rise within me as I was reminded of how religion must tear down the individual before it can offer a solution to the "sin problem." I thought about my conversations of the previous evenings with the New Testament writers. I thought about my relationship with God and how God and I cannot be separated.

I didn't need the material in my hands. However, I knew there were some people in the POD who did. They believed they could be separated from God and they needed a way to reconnect. I decided I would make the material available to those people.

Wednesday, December 15, 2010

As Tuesday night became Wednesday, I struggled staying in the moment. I was looking forward to seeing my attorney on Wednesday. I could place a commissary order on Wednesday, get stuff Thursday, make phone calls, and write on Friday. Library was Wednesday and I needed new reading material. I squirreled away any newspapers I could find so I would have something to read during my time in the cell.

I tried not to suffer with my situation. I thought about why we suffer. I've struggled recently with the definitions of suffering and passion. The two words are often used interchangeably, especially in Christian circles. For example, the suffering of Christ is also called the "Passion of Christ." Our society usually associates suffering with pain and passion with pleasure. It seems odd that these seemingly opposite words are also synonymous.

As I thought about it, I recognized that the key to not suffering was to quit attaching to the results. I wanted out of this situation because this situation wasn't the result I wanted; therefore, I was suffering. If I could quit attaching to the results, I would quit suffering.

This is the connection between passion and suffering. When I am passionate about something, I attach to it. It becomes me. I become it. Therefore, when a new obstacle arises to hinder me in pursuit of my passion, I suffer.

On the other hand, if I release the passion for the result, I release attachment and I don't experience suffering. This doesn't mean that I cease pursuing the goal. It means that I trust God to bring about the result in spite of the obstacle. My job isn't to gain the result. It is to maintain Peace of Mind while I'm having the experience.

Yes, I had a Desire for my family to be reunited, but under what circumstances? Would it be better if we were all together and struggling to move forward or would it be better if we each sought our own path before we came back? Son Two, Daughter One, Son Three and Daughter Two were the bedrocks of our family because they had gone away and come back. I knew they were committed as long as they could grow in the present environment. I now saw that each of us had to do this at some level.

Son One would leave soon. Daughter Three, Daughter Four, and Son Four had been removed. The Wife, always loyal, was committed but I hoped this experience would change her, as it was changing me, so that she too could grow softly strong in her cracked places.

With all of my goals, desires, and passions, I knew the key for me was to stay in this moment and not be attached to the results. Sure, painful things may happen, but I didn't have to suffer with them. I could feel the pain and move to the moment, confident that a divine force was working out a conspiracy for me.

My Attorney didn't show up today. I hoped to see her soon so I could confirm her representation.

I placed my commissary order and begged to borrow two books instead of one from the library. The Monk allowed

74

me to do that because I was such a fast reader. Per his recommendation, I checked out *We're All Doing Time"*. In addition, I borrowed *Proud Spirit* by Rosemary Altea.

Rosemary's books brought me great joy and encouragement. (I say books because on Friday, I found a copy of her book *The Eagle and the Rose*). Her experiences confirmed my message of love without judgment and punishment. Her healing work showed me the wonder of life after death and her openness to spirit challenged the bounds of my belief system.

Thursday, December 16, 2010

My Attorney didn't show up again today. I was beginning to wonder if something was going on with her.

I remembered that My Attorney showed up on Monday due largely to the work of The Hider. The Hider is one of those people that you want on your side in any fight. She came to New Mexico after ruining the careers of her ex-husband and his peers. I suppose other wives have taken down ex-husbands before, but few fell so far as hers. He was a former US Congressman and when she took down him and his peers, they were all serving as State Supreme Court Justices.

Of course, the good ol' boy network in her state didn't let her get by with that. They threatened her life, had her arrested, and disbarred her from practicing law. She had to go on the witness protection program and it offered her so little protection that she fled across the country under an assumed name. She told me the story the first time we talked and I didn't believe her. By the third time we met, she let slip her original name and when I Googled it, scores of hits came up. The poor woman had been through hell. She had written a book to process it but hadn't published it.

I became her accountant and financial advisor. When she ran into issues on her mother's estate, she came to me for counsel. It was one of the greatest compliments I had ever received.

The Hider had helped My Attorney when she ran for office and loved My Attorney's tenaciousness and attitude. I'm sure My Attorney reminded The Hider of herself and The Hider wanted My Attorney to win. The Hider has the skills to run a campaign and had successfully helped a presidential candidate win a state primary by running his campaign.

The Hider loved our family and she would do whatever she could to help us. I was beginning to wonder if My Attorney showed up just to get The Hider to quit bugging her.

My commissary order didn't arrive until bedtime but I was grateful to have it. It was small. Two phone cards, two ink pens, and two legal pads. It was everything I needed for now. I looked forward to tomorrow when I could start writing and call my kids. Life was slowly settling in for me. The staff finally got The Drummer's medication regulated so other than normal nighttime sounds; things were quiet as I went to sleep.

Friday, December 17, 2010

Once again, the quiet didn't last. The early morning hours were interrupted by a new sound: a Jack Black lookalike with a beautiful voice. Upon being placed in his cell, he put his face up against the door and sang songs. His voice was pleasant. He sang on key. He kept changing keys. He sang a long time. When he didn't know the words, he whistled. As with the drumming, I alternated between being wakened and lulled to sleep by the sounds.

I awoke, went through my morning routine, and started writing. I knew there was a chance I could be out by the 24th and I wanted to "catch up" with my daily writing by then. Of course, I needed an attorney to get me through that process and I still didn't have one on retainer. When I was let out of my cell, I called Daughter One.

She told me that My Attorney had received a government job and was closing her practice. In other words, she wasn't taking my case. I told Daughter One to call the other attorney and see if he could come see me on Monday.

I also asked Daughter One to contact Daughter Three's boyfriend because the thirty days ended the next day. After the BSCO showed up on the evening of the November 17th, I requested a meeting with Daughter Three and her boyfriend. He and his dad arrived the next morning and I attempted to talk with them. Before I could finish the first sentence, his dad

79

began to yell at me and call me a fool because I had turned my back on Christ. I allowed him to ramble for a few minutes and attempted to ask him questions. He didn't answer my questions and would only justify his actions for the past 24 hours. It was obvious he wasn't confident about what he had done and he was using his yelling to keep from hearing what I had to say. I remembered when I used to use that technique when I thought I might be wrong and I felt sorry for him. I wondered how many times people had tried to give him advice and he wouldn't listen. I realized there was nothing I could say that would help him understand what I had hoped to tell him.

When he was done, he asked me why I wanted them to visit. I explained that I had hoped to have an intelligent conversation but since that wasn't possible, I believed that, in light of the recent events, it would be best if his son didn't communicate with my daughter for the next thirty days. He told his son he needed to honor that. I have no way of knowing if he did or not. I haven't been in touch with Daughter Three since that day because BCSO told us we could have no contact with the younger three children. I told Daughter Three's boyfriend that, at the end of that time, he could contact me, and we would talk about the next step if he wanted to pursue the relationship with Daughter Three.

Now that those thirty days were over, I wanted to see how he responded under pressure. I wanted to encourage him in his spiritual path by providing him with resources to help him build a healthy, trusting relationship, using his belief system. I knew his belief system. I knew it well because I had lived it for more than thirty-five years. I was not opposed to any of my children following that path because I know those who truly follow it will find love, joy, and peace. All seekers always arrive there. I wanted to communicate forgiveness to him, without judgment. If my experience with his father was any indication, he had never experienced that from a father figure.

I wanted to give him the opportunity to contact me if he wanted to continue the relationship with Daughter Three so I asked Daughter One to tell him I would receive him as a visitor at MDC. Daughter One told me later that she didn't have his phone number so she sent him a private message on Facebook. His only response was to block her and delete her as a friend. I wasn't surprised at his response. I was sure the emotions were still too strong for him to face me.

It was good to talk with Daughter One and good to be able to write. I read *We're All Doing Time* and discovered a remarkable handbook on how to perform a spiritual practice while incarcerated. In addition, I was able to participate in Tai Chi and Yoga classes today. I ended the day tired and fulfilled. I was grateful.

Saturday, December 18, 2010

My second weekend in jail felt almost comfortable, familiar. This concerned me and encouraged me. It concerned me in that I don't believe we should ever be comfortable with anything less than freedom. Freedom is the only way a man can fulfill his destiny and purpose. On the other hand, it excited me in that I felt mentally free. As Mandela said, "My body was in prison but my mind was free."

I picked up two new books last evening. Rosemary Altea's *The Eagle and the Rose* and Elisabeth Kubler-Ross's *The Wheel of Life*. Each book was packed with stories of spiritual growth and challenge. Much to my surprise, both authors wrote openly of spirit guides and how those guides aided their efforts at bringing healing and comfort.

A pattern was emerging in my reading material. Each book I picked up took me deeper into a belief system that I already knew. More than confirming what I already believed, it extended my beliefs into exciting new realms and possibilities. I was beginning to see, really see, God's hand in my life and I was learning to release control. The freedom of losing control was both scary and exhilarating. I could see losing control as a pattern all great leaders followed and I could understand why they would need spirit guides to comfort and console them.

Now that I had reading and writing material, my daily routine was taking shape. I would read, write, and workout while I was in my cell. When I was out of my cell, I would shower, make a phone call, and spend time with the other inmates. Since The Monk wasn't taking medication like the other members of the POD, he had the most capability for conversation. That usually meant I spent time with him. We both liked sports so we would occasionally park ourselves in front of the TV while we talked. Other times, we would walk circles around the POD or around the outside area.

My Saturday afternoon writing was interrupted by Head Counselor's request to chat with me. Head Counselor was a 70ish year-old man with a PhD in something — maybe psychiatry. He had brown eyes and gray hair, including his deeply fuzzy eyebrows and mustache. We discussed the "shadow," and thinking versus knowing. He obviously wasn't comfortable with the details of my case and he felt compelled to work on changing my life perspective.

We talked several times during my stay at MDC and each time, Head Counselor was more forceful in his delivery. He would make a point; tell me he wanted to "go there" with me, and then say, "Talk to me." He usually interrupted my first sentence to make additional points. His listening skills were so poor that dialogue was virtually impossible.

Head Counselor, his peers and interns led the POD's Group meetings and, more often than not, took emotional potshots at the men in the POD. I don't believe the staff was trying to be harmful and I'm not saying the inmates did not receive some benefits from the discussions. I am saying that the staff seemed unclear on what they were attempting to accomplish. Were they trying to make us feel guilty for being in jail? Were they trying to help us make better decisions? Were they just doing time themselves in exchange for a paycheck?

Their brand of traditional mental health treatment identified (diagnosed) the problems without providing solutions. I suspect there maybe solutions available within the treatment. However, they acted as if doing more than casually suggesting them would somehow be wrong or unethical or maybe it would shorten the treatment and the related revenue stream. More than once, the counseling staff would make a suggestion and inmates would ask for more information. Every time, the staff ignored the question. It appeared as if the staff felt like they might work themselves out of a job if they got too many results with the inmates.

Sunday, December 19, 2010

Son Two came to visit me today. It was good to see him and catch up on what was happening with him. I could tell that he was doing everything he could to keep the family finances in order while taking care of his other responsibilities. I could see the stress in his face and I knew he was growing through the process. With his visits and my phone calls with Daughter One, I finally had a communication stream with the outside. That was helpful.

Sunday was much like Saturday. I followed the routine I had established the previous day of reading, writing, and working out while in my cell and watching TV, walking with The Monk, and sharing stories while out of the cell.

Of course, I was still at the mercy of the CO on duty when it came to time in and out of the cell. I was constantly reminding myself that I really couldn't control anything except my attitude. I would discover how important that was the next day.

Monday, December 20, 2010

When I talked to Daughter One today, she told me she had successfully made contact with the attorney over the weekend and he promised to be here today. He didn't show. I had an indictment hearing scheduled in three days and no attorney – or so I thought. Around 12:30, a woman walked in and asked to speak to me. She introduced herself as Substitute Attorney and she said My Attorney sent her. Her resume was impressive. She had worked with the public defender's office, the district attorney's office, and in private practice. In addition, she had been a judge for 14 years. I told her I wanted to retain her because she had at least shown up and I had to trust that she was the person to represent us. She told me she would visit The Wife and then be back in a day or so to do the contract. I told her I would have the kids bring her a blank check so I could pay her when she returned.

This series of events gave me pause to think about how little control we sometimes have over life – at least at a conscious level. Yes, I believe we are 100% responsible for the results in our lives. Yes, I believe we are co-creators with God. However, the "how" of this process is the mystery. We can't force the results or create our life alone. The results only come as we yield to the process without regards to the sensations of pain and pleasure.

Do I want to be here? No. Do I understand that by being here, I will move forward more quickly than before? Yes. Do I know how this will happen? No. Will I yield to this process? Yes, I will because I have no other choice except to mumble and complain about it and I will not do that – except for those brief moments when I forget that isn't my preference.

Jail makes these life lessons obviously clear. The key for me will be to remember that life outside of jail is that way too. We set our paths prior to life and walk them during life. We can make choices that slow or accelerate the journey down those paths. However, if we remain conscious and in the moment, those choices are easy to see and obvious, almost making them something we have to do.

The Monk told me that he heard a voice telling him not to go outside on the morning of his arrest. He went outside anyway and within thirty seconds was in the middle of the drama that led to his arrest. Was the voice the obvious choice or was it his action? It was his action. He knew he was going to be arrested and, like Paul going back to Jerusalem, he went anyway. As a result, The Monk determined he would pursue a spiritual path. Otherwise, according to him he would have remained stuck in a destructive lifestyle.

Looking at my own situation, I purposely sought a path of love and followed it. I trusted those around me to be honest and did what I knew to do. In spite of my intentions and my carefulness, I was arrested. My unconscious desire to explore the next thing after jail propelled me to experience jail. God's plan is big and bold and includes what I'm experiencing now. There are no accidents.

Over the past several days, I had visions and feelings of freedom. I'm in my house, out of this facility, living my life. I must admit that I had similar feelings of jail prior to this experience, so I assume freedom is ahead. These feelings are especially strong during my meditation time when I slip into the dream state between consciousness and unconsciousness. I'm sure God knows what happens next because, from an eternal perspective, everything happens outside of the time dimension so it all happens at the same time.

I bog down when I begin to think about how I'm going to get out. I am free when I allow my mind to be free, no matter where I'm located. I know I can read and write to stay in the moment so I am doing that.

Tuesday, December 21, 2010

Today is a quiet day or the POD. The Drummer is on meds and no longer playing. The same is true for the singer. Several inmates have been released and the ones remaining are quiet and respectful. This is a haven of peace today.

Substitute Attorney did not come to see me today. Daughter One said they delivered the blank check and talked to her, so all is looking good. I look forward to Substitute Attorney's next visit.

The most interesting thing about today was the tidbit of news that The Father-in-Law had sent an email to his friends indicating that he had been trying to find a way to conspire with the authorities to put The Wife and me in jail. This seems unlikely to me. However, the source of the information is reliable so I suppose it could be true. It certainly would explain why he showed up at our house on the 17th about ten minutes after BCSO arrived.

As I think about why The Father-in-Law would do this, I realize he has several motivations. First, based on his belief system, he believes our family is on the path to hell and he wants to bring us to repentance. This is the difference between a religious man and a spiritual one. A religious man thinks he has the answers and he must control other people with those answers. A spiritual man makes observations based on experience while he continues to seek for the appropriate answer for each situation. A religious man points others to himself. A spiritual man points others to within themselves. The Father-in-Law is a religious man with an insatiable desire for control. Putting us in jail is one way he can control us – at least he thinks it is.

The second reason he would do this is that he has a death wish. He has prophesied his immediate demise for more than 25 years and he has voiced his anger at God for not taking him. Since his religion is based on sacrifice, he often looks for ways to "kill himself" by sacrificing his relationships with the current people in his life in exchange for building new relationships with those he can "mentor." His most recent attempt to do this is his jail ministry. Previous attempts included adopting troubled kids, attempting to pastor a church, and a counseling ministry. I could see him planning to be the "sacrificial lamb" for our family by disrupting his life with this situation and reasoning it would be worth it if it brought us to repentance.

His belief system is full of sacrificial acts that he believes bring about a greater good. I understand the philosophy and it looks good on the surface. However, I don't agree with it because, if sacrifice is needed, then God is insufficient. God is the Creator. Therefore, God can and will create whatever is needed. God doesn't need to take from one to give to another. God is capable of giving to all and does give to all, all the time. Mankind's difficulty is in receiving and using those gifts. Once a person learns to do that, the gifts flow and there is no need for sacrifice.

Wednesday, December 22, 2010

Today was another peaceful day in the POD. I talked with Daughter One and, as it turns out, The Father-in-Law's email was just a "request for prayer," something I appreciate. Of course, I'd appreciate it more if he and his religious friends had talked with me prior to all these things happening. I suppose it is true that all the exercise some people get is "running down other people anc jumping to conclusions."

I've known for quite a while that punishment is counterproductive to a healthy society. This experience has given me even more insight in this topic. Being locked up to pay for something done in the past never solves the problem. What I see in MDC is a community of people who understand they've been accused of doing something illegal. Few of them even have the capacity to think about making it right because their freedom to do so has been taken away. Each person spends so much energy on acquiring freedom that he has little energy left to think about restitution or correction.

The longer a person is in custody, the more distance there is between his action and the opportunity to correct it. This current system creates bitter, angry inmates who see no connection between getting out and correcting their behavior. Therefore, the inmate has no desire to correct his action because it isn't directly related to his freedom.

If the system took the same resources it uses now (i.e. the courts, case workers, counselors, and attorneys), and worked to quickly restore inmates to their outside environment based on their ability and demonstrated skill to correct behavior, there would be less time to become bitter and angry. Each inmate would have the opportunity to learn life skills and would be less likely to repeat the action that led to his arrest.

In addition, the adjustment back to society would be easier to make. Many inmates become so accustomed to life in jail that they would rather be here than on the outside. There are several people in this POD who want to be in MDC. They have no family, nowhere to live, no job waiting for them on the outside, and no way to get three meals and a warm bed each evening. Each one has a story of how his first arrest put such a stigma on him that his friends and family didn't want anything to do with him. The goal of the "corrections system" should be correction. Instead, it has become punishment, as much as possible under the law.

The "American way" is described as innocent until proven guilty. However, that is not the case. When a person is arrested, especially in a high profile case such as mine, the guilt is assumed immediately. The arresting authorities imply guilt to justify their actions. The media reports those implications. The public usually believes them. The person is locked up for a period of time and must pay a significant amount of money to be released. If the bond is paid in full, which is seldom the case, it will be returned once the case is resolved. If the more affordable 10% surety is paid, this money is never returned. It goes into the government coffers. It is the punishment a person pays for being charged, even if he is never found to be guilty.

The new American way is "guilty as charged, even if the court system determines innocence sometime in the future."

It is interesting to watch my emotions when someone tells us they are leaving. I always tear up, tell them congratulations, and rejoice. I'm fortunate to be in a "pleasant POD." However, jail is a terrible place to live. It is my opinion that no one should ever be locked up for more than a few days. I suppose there are arguments for some exceptions. However, they pale when compared to the cost to humanity because of this barbaric justice system. When the state locks up someone, it does what would be illegal if a citizen did that to another citizen. The state gives likeminded offenders opportunities to reinforce their belief systems by putting them together. Then, it creates an environment of intimidation by bringing in guards and officers.

A study done at the Stanford University in 1971 demonstrates the destructive forces that are set in motion whenever one group of people has control over another group. College students were assigned the roles of prisoners and guards and they lived in a prison environment. The planned two-week study was ended in six days because of what the situation was doing to the college students who participated. In only a few days, the guards became sadistic and the prisoners became depressed and showed signs of extreme stress.

I see similar results in MDC. The COs, especially the inexperienced ones, are sadistic and demonstrate their fear through taking power trips over the inmates. The inmates have signs of stress on their faces, especially upon returning from court, after talking on the phones with loved ones, or returning from a video visit. In spite of the stress, in my two weeks here,

I've yet to see an altercation other than a couple of brief shouting matches. In each case, only one person was being unreasonable and the situation resolved quickly. The gentlemen in this POD work together, support one another, and cooperate. I believe we would do the same outside this environment. Would we? I'll never have the opportunity to answer that question.

I do know that, as a society, we must decide whether man is intrinsically good or evil. Many religious teachings say we are born into sin and are evil from birth. This leads to beliefs that man must be regulated, and there must be laws to keep man in line. What if the opposite were true? What if man was born holy, pure, and without sin? Or even without the capability to do anything other than what he agreed to do before coming to this lifetime. Would that change the way we live our lives? Would we be able to do away with the legal system? Would we be able to rebuild it so that it is less barbaric and more conducive to quick restoration? The argument against this is that authority systems must protect society. My question is "Who will protect us from the authority systems?"

Every major conflict I've faced in my life came from the authority system that said, "You can't do it that way," even though the way I was doing it was producing results, was legal, and met the stated goals of our task. Even in our current situation, we were building a community based on love and communication. It only broke down when religious authorities and later government authorities said, "You can't do it that way."

As I reflect on this, I see a society driven by morality instead of results. Unfortunately, the current moral system doesn't produce the stated moral results. Instead, it creates more immorality. For example, the corrections system doesn't produce correction. It produces repeat offenders. The church doesn't produce saints. It produces sinners. Each of those "moral systems" focuses so much on the mistakes that the participants learn to make more mistakes instead of correcting them.

I understand that part of this is a marketing strategy that generates repeat business. If the corrections system really corrected, offenders wouldn't return. If the church really produced saints, sinners wouldn't need forgiveness. However, if the focus for these systems was results over morals, there would be plenty of repeat business through referrals and customers coming back to get more of what produces the results they desire. Oh, and by the way, if the corrections and religious systems focused on results, the morals would take care of themselves because the best results happen through the practice of positive activities – what many people would define as morals.

This is typical of any large government-based system. The education system doesn't educate. It babysits and stays away from teaching anything too creative for fear of being persecuted, even when this may not be in the best interest of the student. The medical system doesn't heal. It medicates and practices with great restraint to avoid lawsuits, even when it may not be in the best interest of the patient. These large systems think that if the education system really educated, teachers wouldn't be necessary. They think that if the medical system really healed, doctors wouldn't be necessary. The truth is that those who truly teach and heal attract clients outside of these large government based systems and sometimes must take a risk to do so.

The government believes it must protect its citizens because the citizens are too dumb to protect themselves. The truth is that I am responsible for the results in my life. If the government wants to help me help myself, that could be healthy and productive. However, when the government or any large institution focuses more on what it calls morality than it focuses on results, neither goal is accomplished. The reason is that the focus on morality is always used to control others and one human's control of another is the greatest immoral act.

I still haven't seen Substitute Attorney today. Daughter One said she didn't make it out here yesterday before lockdown but she was coming out here today. My indictment is tomorrow and I understand she will be here for it. I don't know what to expect and that concerns me. I was worried quite a bit about that earlier but feel better now. I assume my subconscious knows what is going on so I'm relaxing into that.

I just finished reading *When Things Fall Apart* by Pema Chodron. I am reminded that this moment is the only path I have. I must walk it, live it, and accept it. Today is an adventure and I will apply myself to it fully, not waiting for another day. One way to do this is through practice of Tonglen. In this meditation exercise, we breathe in the discomfort and breathe out the pleasure. This compassionate exercise encourages moving into all moments without avoiding anything. It allows me to experience pain willingly and convert it to pleasure. This process prevents me from ignoring a painful moment and allows me to stay within it. Most pain comes from fear of "what's next?" By leaning into the pain, I experience it fully and learn the insight instead of worrying about the next moment. The goal isn't to reduce the pain. It is to experience it but not suffer with it.

I'm now reading *The Sacred Hoop* by Paula Gunn Allen. This book reminds me that the whole idea of whether man is born good or evil has its roots in patriarchal vs. matriarchal societies. Patriarchal, western, Christian/Jewish/Muslim societies tend to see humanity as evil. Matriarchal, tribal societies tend to see humanity as good. The reasoning is simple. In a patriarchal society, man is aggressive rather than nurturing. This creates an imbalance that puts the aggressive male in an aggressive role. This produces an imbalance of aggression and results in a greater tendency for war. In a matriarchal society, women are aggressive and men nurture. This puts each sex in a role that balances the natural tendency. This balance between the sexes allows for a peaceful environment and culture.

The author says that taboo means sacred and the reason we avoid taboos is because of the power held within these practices. For example, a menstruating woman has an increased level of spiritual power over a non-menstruating one. Therefore, man put taboos on this event. This is especially true with the Jewish/Christian/Muslim traditions.

Thursday, December 23, 2010

My indictment was scheduled for today. No one came to get me. No one took me to the indictment. At the end of the day, I had no information about it. If I'm not indicted, I can leave tomorrow. If I am indicted, there will be more uncertainty.

I've had visions of the indictment paperwork being mishandled and the case not being heard. I can only hope at this point, especially after my conversation with Substitute Attorney. She finally arrived yesterday afternoon during lockdown. She apologized for taking several days to arrive. I think she is overwhelmed by our case but still wants to take it. I'm sure she will do well with it. Of course, that doesn't guarantee any results.

We talked about the case and my goals. I learned about the laws regarding my charges and the potential punishments. I explained to her that my perspective of this situation is that it is a miracle, a divine plan to give me the opportunity to write and address issues important to me, my family, my community, and our culture. I could see her trying to wrap her brain around building a defense for a client who wants to write a book about his experience before the trial. I could see the doubt in her eyes about whether she really wanted to do this.

Substitute Attorney promised to check on the indictment status and relay the message to Daughter One. I was going to call Daughter One last night but I wasn't allowed out of my cell. The new CO (P) was afraid of me and would barely open the door to give me dinner. Her fear was severely over the top. I could imagine her being sadistic if given the opportunity.

After dinner, I thought about the actions that led to my arrest. I'm sure people will judge and condemn my parenting techniques. I'm OK with that. My goal is to raise responsible, intelligent humans who are free of barriers to love. To me, love is the highest calling for each of us. Every issue that we face in our society comes from an absence of love. If we methodically recognize those barriers and consciously remove them, we can create a more loving environment and resolve the issues of the day.

I believe this starts with each individual. We each have powerful barriers to love. Unfortunately, many of those barriers are rooted in our attitudes about sex. Sex isn't love although it certainly can be an expression of love. Sex is a conscious act that happens between consenting individuals. It is powerful emotionally, physically, and spiritually. My opinion is that the reason there are so many laws and taboos against certain varieties of sex is that the authorities, both religious and government, recognized these powers and were afraid of them.

This is not just my opinion. Every document I've read that addresses this topic says the same thing whether it was written this year, ten years ago, hundreds of years ago, or thousands of years ago. People who were open in their sexuality experienced a freedom and power other people didn't experience. The other people were afraid of the sexual openness; therefore, they persecuted and punished those who were open. Sometimes these were called witch trials. Sometimes this was called converting the savages to religion.

Sometimes this was called slavery. Sometimes this was called the inquisition.

Because the beginning of a healthy sexual relationship consists of loving actions, some acts of love, especially touch, are classified as sexual acts by religion and the courts. Therefore, they are discouraged or labeled illegal. Is it acceptable for a parent to hug a child? Is it acceptable for a non-parent adult to hug a child? Is t acceptable for two friends of the opposite sex to hug without being accused of having an affair? Is it acceptable for two friends of the same sex to hug without being accused of being homosexual? What if someone kisses a friend on the cheek or, even "worse," on the lips?

These socially unacceptable actions are simply acts of love. However, because they are criticized by some parts of society, people are afraid to practice acts of love. This creates barriers to love. Each individual needs love. However, the fear of expressing and meeting that need produces a society that avoids love and evolves into doing something else.

In fact, society's paranoia over sex has evolved to the point that we are more comfortable with violence than we are with sex. Our theatres are filled with movies depicting violent acts of destruction including murder and war. These acts are considered normal and viewed with acceptance as real life events. However, if those same movies have a loving sex scene that shows any nudity or detail, they are criticized and labeled as evil and perverted.

Our western, male-dominated society honors the taking of life, while punishing and ridiculing those who wish to honor the creating of life.

Friday, December 24, 2010

I'm spending Christmas Eve in jail. I've always struggled with the holidays. I previously thought it was the commercialization or the Christianizing of the pagan holiday. It has always seemed fake to me and only recently have I come to accept it as a time of love and celebration. I was actually looking forward to this year's holiday because, for the first time in many years, we had money in the bank and could take a few days off without wondering about cash flow. Now, I suspect that part of my struggle with the day had to do with my subconscious knowing I'd be locked up over a Christmas holiday. This becomes bitterer as I think about next weeks' trip that will not happen. The Wife and I will be married 25 years on January 1, 2011 and, unless a miracle happens, we'll spend it apart in jail.

We planned to go to New York City, stay for three nights, watch the ball drop in Times Square, and go to a Broadway Show. We made reservations last February and had looked forward to the trip all year. Now....I cried when I realized it wouldn't happen. We'll go another year. I just don't know which one yet. I do know we'll get out of here and find a place of gratitude, joy, and peace while we live our passion. And, I know we'll live fuller than we lived before jail.

Head Counselor has shown an interest in me over the past few days. My contribution to Group has obviously stimulated Head Counselor to some exciting thoughts. Two days ago, he brought up a sports topic. I'm an only child, so sports are my siblings. I had plenty to say about the topic. He said he was impressed with my knowledge.

Yesterday, we were discussing taking responsibility for our actions and I asked what he meant by that. Did he mean doing time or making amends? He was blown away by the question and it became the focal point of conversation for the rest of Group. When we finished, he came to me and said my comments made him feel like he was in a university setting. In the next Group, he gave each of us a word to describe us. Mine was "intellect."

I found that interesting. In fact, everyone I've talked with in here comments on my intelligence. Maybe I'm think too much. As Bill Gothard says, "One step ahead makes you a leader. Ten steps ahead make you a martyr."

Is that the reason for my arrest? Was I so far ahead of the norm that it made people uncomfortable? What I was doing with our family was implementing a way for us to express love *without sexual overtures*. Those actions, from religious perspectives, were interpreted as sexual. Religious leaders, afraid of the power of sexual energy, feel a need to prevent anyone from learning about this power. Therefore, they must regulate and control how we express love with one another. If anything hints of sexual activity, it must be regulated.

In *Conversations with God*, the author uses the term "synergistic energy exchange" as a definition of sex. (From this point forward, I use "S.E.X." when referring to this term and "sex" when referring to a more traditional definition for sex.) S.E.X. permeates everything we do. While the sex act can certainly be a synergistic energy exchange, there are many other activities that fall within this description of S.E.X.

This goes back to what I wrote earlier about sexual energy not having to be used for sexual activity, especially when the agreement is to use it for something else. Loving touch always brings about energy. This may be sexual arousal or, more likely, it is a feeling of contentment, companionship, and connection. Either way, it is certainly S.E.X.ual and overcomes the barriers to love.

This is the goal for how I live my life. I can't see how to compromise my call to bring peace by sharing love, even if the result is criminal charges and jail time. As Rosemary Altea says, "I must respect myself. I must live what I believe, must live all that I believe and teach or I am nothing and of no value to myself."

My arrest gives me clarity on how I teach what I teach. It shows me that the opposition to love, especially openness and nakedness, whether emotional, mental, or physical is severe. Our police state opposes it, even though it is legal. My arrest shows me that I must put certain things in place to protect my legal right to teach the truth. I will need to put an attorney on retainer. I will need to have clients sign releases. I will have to limit my teachings to those who are 18 or older.

My teachings through The Peace of Mind Training Institute are powerful. They are life changing. They are world changing. I need to understand that the old way of thinking will fight these teachings. This is a part of history and it is a part of today. However, if we do it wisely this time, we can create a more loving world, one that doesn't have to suffer an apocalyptic meltdown during the prophesied coming change.

Elisabeth Kubler Ross says, "It is impossible to live life at the highest level unless you get rid of your unfinished business." I had unfinished business with this situation because I had not taken the legal steps necessary to insure my freedom while teaching. I will take those steps. In addition, I have unfinished financial business. I know I can resolve that given enough time. With those two issues resolved, I'll move forward at the highest level soon. I sense the time approaching.

The Drummer went back to his drums last night. The female CO who was afraid of me (P) went to his cell, unlocked the door and yelled "Excuse me." I don't know what she said afterwards but he quit playing. I noticed The Drummer was removed from Group this morning. I'm not in Group today. B, today's CO, usually lets me out for lunch around 10 and allows me to be out until lockdown at 2. The normal Group session starts at 8:30.

The other daytime COs aren't as generous yet. They allow me to attend Group sometimes, and they give me enough time to shower, make a phone call, etc. However, they usually only allow me a couple hours of time out of my cell. The evening COs give me even less freedom. I'm lucky to get out for 30 minutes and usually have to eat dinner in my cell. The weekend CO lets me out for dinner and I can stay out until lights out. Otherwise, I'm in my cell a long time. I would have been in from 11:30 AM until lights out yesterday if Substitute Attorney had not visited. We have library on Monday, Wednesday and Friday so can get out long enough to exchange books.

I sat outside in the sun for a while today and talked with The Monk and an inmate I'll call Forrest Gump. The Monk was informative and helpful as always. Forest was just funny. He must be from the south because he has a habit of making certain one syllable words into two syllable ones. Dumb becomes de-um and socks becomes su-ocks. He stutters and talks slowly. He is a nice guy to chat with and he seems like he is always high on something. At first, I thought it was his medication. Then, I realized, he is proud of being dumb because it means he isn't competent to stand trial. Of course, he is still in jail so maybe he doesn't have all the facts on his situation. One thing he does know, that has been confirmed by other inmates; he was beaten in another POD and he has a lawsuit pending against MDC. I can believe he got in a fight somewhere. He has a short temper and is quick to complain about things. I watched him and The Vulture almost get into it a couple times over the past few days.

Speaking of The Vulture, he was released a few days ago but he's already back. He has not been allowed in the commons area since his return and Head Counselor says he is going to move him somewhere else and not let him disrupt what is going on here.

What is going on here is mostly a positive Group therapy environment. There are 25 or so men who are waiting for the court system to get to our cases. The Monk told me today that it works like this. They indict you. Then in 2-3 weeks, you can plead guilty or innocent. If guilty, you go to sentencing. If innocent, you wait about six months until they offer a plea bargain. If you reject it, they have three months to offer a second one. If you reject it, you go to trial. The Monk has decided to stay here a year and wait it out. He has relatives who could bail him out, but he won't ask them to do that.

As for me, my bond is too high to bail out so we're looking at attempting to reduce it at the upcoming hearing. It may be wishful thinking but it's my only option at this time. Of course, this is a moot point if it turns out I wasn't indicted yesterday.

While waiting for all of this to happen, Head Counselor is working with us on processing emotions, responsibility, and all the other things that lead to positive mental health. The example he sets for us in dealing with the difficult inmates is the opposite of what he teaches in the Group settings so there is a mixed message. He teaches us to negotiate, talk slowly, and reach agreements without dominating the other person. Then, when an inmate is difficult, he treats them harshly and tells them he is in control of the POD and they must follow his rules. I understand the need for staff to be dominant in a jail setting. However, his walk and talk don't match so it tells the inmates that he doesn't believe what he teaches because he doesn't practice it. Even Forest Gump commented on the "do as I say not as I do" philosophy. Maybe Forest isn't so dumb after all.

In spite of Head Counselor's inability to practice what he preaches, he demonstrates compassion and courage in his role. Without his compassion, he would fail miserably at his task because of his contradictions. The reason is that he is a Christian believer who believes in judgment, practicing modern psychology which doesn't encourage judgment. He attempts to be loyal to his beliefs and his practice so he often contradicts himself. He doesn't seem to know that the underlying philosophies behind his belief and his practice are at odds with each other so he isn't conscious of how confused he is at times, although his face certainly shows it. It is a classic example of him not yet thinking through his root beliefs. If he struggles too much, I've learned to ask questions to help "right his ship" at least for the current Group session. I don't do it for him. I do it to help the inmates who often hang on every word he says. I'm sure his confusion doesn't hep some of the men in here especially those who are looking for answers.

In addition to Head Counselor, there are other counselors, interns, and medical professionals on staff. They do "case plans" so we can be ready to go back into society. They give us TB tests so we can't have a TB outbreak in MDC. They provide daily meds.

On occasion, we'll have a second or third rover in the POD. These people have one job: Sit outside a cell and make sure the inmate doesn't commit suicide. Inmates on suicide watch either wear red suits (instead of orange) with "HIGH RISK" stenciled on the back or some kind of funky Velcro latched blanket. There are two degrees of suicide watch. One that requires a guard and one that does not. I pity the guards who have that duty. They cannot move out of the sight of the inmate, who is usually doing nothing but sleeping. These rovers are more confined than the inmates.

The people who make this POD run are the mentors. This POD has four and each one has a level of maturity and grace that makes it difficult for me to see them as inmates. It is only when I see the worry and stress in their faces that I remember they have legal issues too. In fact, I'll be amazed if anyone who is in here, just waiting, doesn't acquire significant maturity and grace. This doing time stuff is stressful. My fellow inmates escape through eating, sleeping, and meds. Me, I escape through reading, writing, and talking when I can be in the commons area. We get a newspaper every day, so I use it to kill a couple hours. I devour the sports and comics. I also do the puzzles. It keeps my mind active.

I keep going back to what Ralph Waldo Emerson said, "There is a crack in everything God has made." I agree with that. I think that the crack adds character and gives us a point of focus. As I grow softly strong in my cracked places, I have to use this experience to ask, "What can I learn?" How can I grow? "How strong can I become?"

One of my "cracks" is a struggle with love. This goes back to my childhood and some of the people I wanted to "love" who didn't love me back. I developed a coldness so that I wouldn't give my heart to anyone. Instead, I set up conditions for relationships and eliminated those who didn't meet the conditions. This is a good way to pick clients and business associates. It isn't a good way to learn how to love.

I've made significant progress in this area over the past few months and I sense a shift inside of me that will serve me well when I leave this place. I cry for joy when a man receives his freedom. My heart aches when I see the men in here facing this barbaric judicial system. I'm conscious that I have a love and compassion for these men that I never had before.

Another crack is that I forget to "be" and, instead, feel like I must "do." There isn't that much to do in here so "being" becomes necessary. I can take my time with every task and do it well. In fact, taking my time to pay attention to every detail is one thing that helps me pass the time. For example, personal cleanliness has become important to me because I don't currently have access to deodorant. Therefore, when I exercise in the morning and again in the afternoon, I take my shirt off so

I don't "stink it up" and then take a sponge bath afterward. I'm motivated to keep my shirt clean because I only get fresh clothes on Sunday and Thursday. Upon completion of the sponge bath, I then use the only paper product I have available, toilet paper, to clean the stainless steel sink area until it is spotless.

After every meal at my stainless steel desk, I do the same thing. I follow up by brushing my teeth. These are the little things that become important. They show me I can be civilized in a barbaric setting. I know that I will be more conscious of these little chores when I leave MDC and will consider them important. I'll take the time to do them because I won't see myself as too busy to do them. I somehow feel like I will perceive that life will slow down when I leave MDC. I think I'll have just as much to do but my experience will allow me to see it differently.

After finishing *The Sacred Hoop*, I recognized that I was using the wrong term earlier. Tribes are not matriarchal. They operate via a gynocracy where the women lead the culture. Women-led cultures have almost no incidence of rape because they encourage a free and easy sexuality. Alternative lifestyles, other than the nuclear family of one man, one woman and their children, are encouraged, even honored, so that prejudice and discrimination are almost non-existent. There is an equal sharing of goods so there is no need to steal. In addition, with the absence of harmful actions, punitive measures aren't necessary. If someone makes a mistake, they are corrected so that harmful barbaric techniques aren't used, perpetuated, and taught to society. As 16th century explorer Peter Martyr wrote, it is "a country where there are no soldiers, no gendarmes or police, no nobles, kings, regents, prefects, or judges, no prison, no lawsuits... All are equal and free."

Can such a society exist? I believe it must if we are to experience Peace on Earth. That seems to be quite profound a statement on this Christmas Eve.

Saturday, December 25, 2010

Christmas in jail really isn't that different from any other day. It is early as I write so I can only suppose there will be random acts of kindness today. I wait and see.

I keep thinking about what I could have done to avoid jail. So far, I can think of nothing I could have done differently while remaining in integrity with who I am. I am an open, loving, accepting human being with nothing to hide. I did not hurt my children or force them to do what they didn't want to do. However, my actions are being called "illegal." There are times when I've silently screamed, "This isn't fair!" and then I remember that when things don't make sense, when things are unfair, a miracle is at work and it is appropriate for me to lean into the process and experience it fully.

The reader may wonder why openness is so important to me. The primary reason is that openness is how we learn. My parents were so afraid to talk about sex that I can only remember two pieces of instruction from them. Mom's was "Don't get a girl pregnant." Dad's was "That's it." A comment he made after a bull mounted a cow on my uncle's farm. At the time, I didn't even recognize what "it" was. When I got to college, I knew so little about sex that my health class was quite informative.

The Wife's experiences with sex education were similar. Any discussion her parents had about sex had to be done with the lights off, using code words. Her biggest complaint about her childhood was the lack of openness in her family with religion, money and politics, the three things you should "never talk about." She felt unprepared for life because she couldn't participate in significant conversation topics.

Even as adults, our parents wouldn't discuss crucial life topics with us. She and I decided things would be different with our kids. We talked about anything and everything. That may have made the kids uncomfortable at times but they're better equipped for life than we were.

Daughter Two came to visit yesterday and she asked great questions about what they need to do with various business and family responsibilities. Son Two and Daughter One do that every time I talk with them. I hate to think about how difficult this would be if we had not talked to them openly about so many topics.

Looking back, I can see that Son One's Partner had trouble accepting this openness in our family. After reading *The Sacred Hoop,* I understand that this openness may only come if the females step forward and become assertive in leadership while the men focus on nurturing. Son One's Partner prefers to be rescued and submit to a man. However, I see that she has a desire, currently hidden to her at the conscious level, to become assertive and participate in an open and loving family. I'm confident there will be a move back to New Mexico in the future. It may be 5 to 10 years but I think it will happen as she becomes more confident in who she is.

There are times when I suppose I "should" feel remorse for being in jail. At those times I'm reminded not to "should myself" (shit myself) and that I'm in here because I have a different belief system, a system that runs contrary to the punitive, patriarchal system that rules this realm. I could worry about my criminal record but then I think, "Why does a blemish on a record matter when the record keeping system has significant flaws in its foundation?"

I recognize that I have lost certain freedoms as a result. I see that I may be ostracized. That's nothing new. Other people have often seen me as "different." I am different because I believe I can talk directly to God. I am different because I believe the world is an abundant place. I am different because I believe that man is naturally good. I don't mind being ostracized for those reasons.

There is a sorting process we all go through. During this sorting process, some people stay and others leave. My arrest is part of my sorting process. There were people in my life that were energy takers; those who wanted me to perform tasks for them but didn't want to pay for those tasks. Daughter One had told me that they were the first ones to leave and no longer want to do business with me.

I had thought this book would keep me occupied through my two weeks in jail. Now that this time will be longer, I know I must find other projects to keep me occupied. I've thought about writing other books, outlining new seminars for Peace of Mind Training Institute, and other projects like body building, deep meditation, and trance work. It will be interesting to see where I go with these options.

There was a second Group session yesterday that took place after I was out of my cell. The topic was grief and loss. During that time, we learned that one of our fellow inmates lost a son last week. I admire this man and his strength. I see him and a buddy studying the Bible together every night. I don't know what their charges are but they seem like they don't belong here so I suspect domestic violence.

Please allow me to explain.

I have noticed that many of the men who are in MDC on domestic violence charges are pleasant men. They communicate easily. They smile. They encourage other people. If they talk about the situation that led to their arrest, the story is almost always the same. It goes like this. "My woman got mad at me, went off on me, and called the cops."

"Did you hit her?"

"No, I know better. I put up my arms to keep her from hitting me and when that didn't work, I held her arms but I didn't hit her."

I realize I'm only hearing one side of the story. Still, one thing is certain. All a woman has to do is call the cops and say a man has hit her and the man goes to jail. This is not an exaggeration. I had heard this story many times prior to coming to jail. Now, I hear it almost every day.

As I wrote earlier, our society runs as a male-dominated police state. The underlying message is that man "owns" his family and must protect them. He forgets to nurture because he is busy protecting and a man cannot nurture while he is defending. Nurturing is opposite of defending and it is impossible to do opposite acts at the same time.

This attitude of protection forces the man to believe he must be in control of his household. With this attitude, a man does not respond in a nurturing manner when someone, even a family member, challenges him. Instead, he responds by defending himself and his possessions. He believes this is the only way he can protect his possessions. Of course, if a violent action or an implied violent action towards his family members is reported to the police, he is usually arrested.

When a man is arrested, this reinforces the idea that force is the best way to resolve conflicts. Instead of learning nurturing skills, the man learns that when things get tough, violence and force, rather than discussion and love, are the tools to bring resolution. This is the consequence of living in our current male-dominated police state where a man can be threatened.

In a society where women lead and are honored, man cannot be threatened. He has nothing to lose, nothing to protect or defend; therefore, a man is less likely to become violent. According to Paula Gunn Allen, author of *The Sacred Hoop,* domestic violence is virtually non-existent in a gynocracy. However, in our male dominated society, it is so common that the authorities use it as an excuse to arrest many men, even when little violence has taken place. In many cases, loud words can qualify as a threat and result in an arrest for domestic violence.

It is for these reasons that I say I suspect these two men are in here for domestic violence charges.

The session on grief and loss was counterproductive to most of the inmates. There was minimal participation except to tell Head Counselor we would rather ignore our loss than process it. The one exception was an inmate who is the proverbial Sad Sack, carrying around an emotional wet blanket, and telling his story to anyone who will listen. It is a story of losing everything and no one loving him. He is his story.

Some people get stuck in a story loop so deeply that it becomes their identity. This is Sad Sack. He is so far into it that no amount of therapy, conversation, or treatment will bring him out of it. He can get out only by choosing a new path. I see it, Head Counselor sees it, and PAC 2 Psychiatrist sees it. We've all told him the same thing. Other inmates see it too and each of us attempts to help him away from his story but it has become his identity and he is afraid that if he gives up his story, he will give up his identity and he will lose who he is.

I appreciated the fact that Head Counselor thought he could help inmates process the loss of not being with family on Christmas Eve. However, it was clear that he didn't think through the emotional duress he initiated by doing so. The sadness in the eyes of each inmate was overwhelming. I watched as the sadness became anger. I was concerned it would become violence. The inmates did not process the grief. They ignored it. I believe he would have done far more for the emotional state of the inmates by bring in some candy and initiating a small celebration.

I've noticed that The Monk looks out for me and connects a little more each day. He now reads outside my door, in the commons area instead of at his bunk. He makes sure I have reading material when I can't get to the library. PAC 2 Psychiatrist brought him some books yesterday. I now have two of them in my room. It is good to have a friend "on the inside."

The Monk and I chatted yesterday about a concept called "criminal think." He said they had discussed it during a Group when I was in my cell. Criminal think is a way of thinking that someone develops to survive tough times. A person develops a rationale to steal, hurt others, and lie because they think it is necessary to do this to survive. Many inmates function this way; therefore, I have learned to take a step back from them. (Now that I think about it, I realize many people practice "criminal think" on the outside too and I respond by avoiding them.)

Most people practice criminal think subtly. The Vulture does it openly. Now that he is back, the entire POD has rejected him. (Head Counselor had promised that The Vulture wouldn't be allowed into general population but he didn't keep that promise.) As a result of the rejection, The Vulture acts out more. He tries to steal food at meals. He is loud. He is pushy.

The Drummer also practices criminal think openly. Besides his drumming, he rips Bibles apart and throws food at his cell window. He hurts so he attempts to hurt others. I am reminded that everything is an act of love or a cry for love. I see many cries for love every day.

Many of these guys want to leave but they do the opposite of what they need to do to leave. Poor behavior results in inmates being confined to their cells. In some cases, these guys are so obnoxious the sergeant must come in to supervise their showers. The theory is that criminal think causes people to commit crime. My observation is that humans practice was is called criminal think when threatened and being in jail pushes people into criminal think. It is another way the justice system isn't just and corrections system doesn't correct.

The shower remains a daily luxury for me. Today's was especially significant. I was weepy this morning. A combination of factors including the book I'm reading and the holiday had an emotional impact on me. As I stepped into the flow of the water, it washed away those emotions. I saw them going down the drain and by the time it was over, I was a new man. I love shower therapy!

Today's conversations with The Monk were a great way to kill the time. He told me about a summer trip from Texas to Vancouver that he took as a young man. He hitchhiked most of the trip, did a lot of camping, and had a great time. He also told me about his "crime." A man came after him saying, "I'm going to kill you. I'm going to kill you." and The Monk shot him. He didn't kill the man. He shot him in the arm and leg and he says he would do it again in the same situation.

Since The Wife and I met, this is the longest we have been without talking to each other. We have been together so long that we often don't talk directly with one another. We just "know" what the other person wants or needs and we do it. I wonder how that will change when we're out of here. I miss her and our conversations. We can relay messages to one another through the kids but it isn't the same.

We were apart from each other four months before our wedding. She left at the beginning of September and we were married January 1. I hope the current separation is shorter.

I'm reminded that no matter how long this process takes, I will face it better with gratitude. Today I'm thankful for books to read, something to write, conversation with The Monk, basketball on TV, and a family who loves and supports me even if we can't be together. In addition, it helps to remember this is part of a "Conspiracy for Me" and I can live with purpose by demonstrating love and gratitude every day.

Part of my struggle today has come from wondering about the future. When will I leave MDC? Will I be sentenced? Will the state accept a plea bargain? When will the family be together again? Will all of us ever be together again at one time? Will we figure out a way to keep our finances in order? There are so many questions and all of them are about the future. I recognize that my struggles today are the result of getting out of the moment and focusing on something that isn't here yet. To maintain peace, I must not think about the future and not think about the future.

I'm currently reading Bo Lazoff's *It's a Meaningful Life – It Just Takes Practice*, a book about spiritual practice. He writes about a time in his life when he overcame fear by saying, "Anything that may happen to a human being may happen to me today, and I accept the truth of this." Bill Gothard calls it "yielding rights." It is the understanding that we live in a world of pure potential where anything is possible. This may be something like winning the lottery, losing a loved one, meeting a soul mate, or being arrested. Our goal is to face it with courage, honor, joy, peace, and ove.

When I accept the reality of pure potential, it is important to remember there is one God, one Universe. It was important to The Wife and me to go to New York for our 25th wedding anniversary. However, it was more important to God that we not go. The same God that put us together for 25 years decided we should not celebrate in New York, so we won't.

Sunday, December 26, 2010

There is an emotional relief now that Christmas has passed. I feel this relief every year whether I'm in jail or not. As of this morning, I see clearer what my days are about. I must consciously connect with God and then reach out to those around me.

Previously, I was meditating/praying from a prone position. The guards assumed I was sleeping so they never interrupted me. As of a couple days ago, I've begun meditating in a lotus (cross legged) position. Surprisingly, this gets the guards attention. The first time I did this, the evening guard unlocked my door and told me to come out of my room. This morning, a guard stepped in and asked me if I was OK. I nodded yes to him. Truthfully, I'm more than OK. I find that meditation position to be comfortable and the time goes by quickly. The key is having something to sit on so that the knees are below the hips instead of even with them.

Being in the psych POD is an interesting experience, especially when certain inmates act out. The newest entertainer is The Screamer. At various times of the days and nights, he screams profanities. At least they sound like profanities. His speech is always slurred, like he is on a 24 hour drunk. Most of the guards can't open the door for his meals without a major conflict and, since his cell doesn't have a chuck door, they have to open the main door.

The Drummer's behavior has changed. He cries for food and, when he receives it, he throws it against his door. He did that twice yesterday. The Vulture continues to annoy people by nagging them for any kind of attention – good or bad.

I learned more about The Monk's history yesterday. He had told me previously about a foot injury that causes him to walk with a limp. He actually came within a split second of death. He was working below an eight foot high loading dock when an untrained forklift operator lost his load. The huge solid metal pipes rolled off the dock and crushed his foot. He was kneeling just prior to the event so his heel took the impact. The pipe broke every bone in his foot. Had his coworker not warned The Monk, the pipe would have landed on his head. With the warning, he was able to throw all of his body forward of the impact point except for his foot.

He went to one of the top hospitals in Dallas and the doctors did amazing work. In fact, many hospitals might have chosen to amputate the foot. As it is, he has significant scar tissue, but his foot is fully functional. His foot has grown softly strong in the cracked places.

It is interesting to watch the attitude of the COs. The regular ones are cool. They do their jobs and have nothing to prove with most of us. The rovers who give the regular COs their breaks are totally different. They have huge egos and they do everything by "the book" or maybe I should say by "their book."

Last night, W came in as a rover. Within 10 minutes, he had temporarily locked down the POD for watching a movie. It didn't matter to me, I was already in my cell but it seemed outrageous. Their behavior supports my theory that most people in law enforcement are control freaks. They have to be in charge of somebody or something.

Would this system work better if we were in love with each other? Not just in love with family or spouse or friends, but in love with everyone, looking each person in the eye as we interact with him or her. Of course, it would work better. We would see God in each person and know how to reach out to that person.

The Monk and I talked a lot last night about helping those less fortunate than ourselves. He was doing that when he got into trouble. He decided to help a man with lodging expenses and food because he had a restraining order against him and could not live in his own house. The man had mental issues and a violent past. Still, The Monk wanted to help him. Then, the man turned on The Monk and he shot him in self-defense. How would Jesus have responded to that situation? How would Buddha have responded? Would these great spiritual masters have helped these people? I think of Jesus saying, "The poor will always be with you." I think of Jesus not healing unless he asked permission or someone asked him for healing.

I wonder if the lesson is only to help those who truly want help. I've noticed that if someone is in a situation, that is where he wants to be. For example, when The Drummer throws food and gets put into isolation that is where he wants to be. If The Screamer fights with the CO every time his door is opened and the CO responds by not letting him out of his cell, The Screamer wants to be in his cell. If The Vulture does things that cause those in the POD to reject him, he wants to be rejected. If a person is sick, he wants to be sick. If a person is poor, he wants to be poor.

If I'm in jail, this is where I want to be.

It's a humbling thought until I realize there are many benefits to this experience. I can use what I learn to educate others. I can write this book. I can develop spiritual practices that I wouldn't have developed otherwise. At some level: conscious, subconscious, or super-conscious, I wanted this experience because I knew it would benefit me.

Therefore, when I am given opportunities to help another person, I must consider whether I'm shortcutting his experience, an experience he needs to have to become who he is. I can certainly choose to help. However, I don't have to do so to demonstrate love.

I believe this is the definition of trusting others. Trust doesn't mean that I blindly allow another person to invade my life. It means that I observe his actions and trust his actions to show me who he is. If he doesn't act with integrity, I can trust that he isn't in integrity with himself and I am not disappointed with that.

I notice that many people grumble and complain when someone or some institution doesn't act with integrity. For example, I see a lack of integrity within the corrections/ law enforcement system. It is easy for an individual to feel like a victim when placed inside this system. However, when I recognize that the system doesn't act with integrity, I am not disappointed in those actions because the system is just being what it is.

This helps me remember that I can't control what happens to me. I can only control my responses. Likewise, I can't control what other people do and, unless they really want help, I can't improve their situations. I can only respond to them, ask questions, observe, and assist them in their quest if I choose to do so, if it is in integrity with who I am.

Speaking of integrity, Head Counselor has asked us to speak affirming statements to one another. In spite of this, he comes in every day and says, "I have to tell you, this is the ugliest group of guys I've ever seen." It is a joke. Everyone understands it is a joke. However, I see pain in the eyes of the inmates every time he says it. I feel a dagger turn in my heart every time he says it. I need to talk to him about this.

Daughter One told me that The Wife has been moved from POD 4 (psych) to a segregation POD. That means she is rooming with two other people in a 7 x 14 cell. She's lost 15 pounds and is still stressed. I had hoped she would process this situation and come to peace with it. I know different people have different capacity but I assumed she would use this time to practice what she knows. Maybe she doesn't know it yet. I'm sure I could help her with this but we can't talk so I'll accept the pure potential of the moment and send light and love in her direction.

Today was a day to watch football, so that's what I did. My state of mind is better today and I feel strong. I'm ready to stay here. I'm ready to get out. I'm ready for the day, whatever it brings.

The Drummer was finally let out of his room today. The Screamer was not. He continues to wake five or six times in a 24 hour period to scream obscenities. Several of the other inmates are doing little things to annoy The Vulture. I heard through the grapevine (a CO actually) that he has been booked into MDC 30 times. The latest booking was for something serious so he will be here a while.

Some people want to be in here. There are at least three people in here who say that. They have nowhere to go and nothing to do once they're out of here. They at least have food and shelter in here, so they want to stay.

Daughter One told me we still don't know about the indictments, so it is possible I could leave tomorrow. One part of my being is excited about that but I don't want to anticipate, especially after the emotions of the past two days. I have always been able to trust my intuition, but I'm not sure I'm hearing it when it comes to legal matters. That's an interesting observation. I remember the lesson I learned about intuition a couple years ago.

My life is an on again-off again love affair with intuition. I wish I could trust my intuition completely. The problem is that my intuition was wrong one time, when I was 6 years old so, I don't trust it. Since that 1968 experience, I overanalyze every feeling, every emotion to see if it is right or wrong.

As a little boy, I developed a crush on a cute little girl in my class. I'll call her The Crush. We went through school together from second grade through graduation and the feelings remained. I never acted on it because, in my mind, The Crush was out of my league.

I didn't know her very well, so there was no logical reason for the crush. We seldom talked and when we did, it was about class assignments. It was purely business. Our social paths never crossed because I was in band and choir and The Crush was a cheerleader. My feelings never changed and my inability to act on them taught me my intuition could be wrong.

Every so often, my parents would ask me if I ever heard from The Crush. They knew about my crush and they sensed it was still there. Even after I married and had a family, my parents still asked. Their questions reminded me that my intuition could not be trusted.

I wrote my first book and, in it, I taught that Desires can always be trusted because they are from God (Desire means "of the Father"). I explained that ntegrity is spirituality without exception.

Still, there was a lingering doubt in the back of my mind. I had a crush on The Crush and we didn't even know each other. I tried to write it off as a mistake, something to correct. However, it wouldn't leave.

Then, in November 2008, I joined several social internet sites. My intent was to establish networks to market my writings. The friend requests arrived from acquaintances, classmate, and clients. I recognized all but one. I researched this person and discovered we were in school together. Could it be her?

We traded greetings. I discovered it was The Crush. The old feelings returned. I was so excited I told my friends and family about it. I told my parents I had heard from The Crush. They didn't say much. They seemed to know this would happen.

We traded a few more messages. Once again, the communication was "purely business." It was like old times. The communication reminded me that my intuition could be wrong. I tried not to think about it. I tried to put it behind me. I was successful doing this on the conscious level. However, I discovered the doubts still lingered on the subconscious level.

Finally, I decided to give my intuition another chance. I wrote and sent the following email.

Being in touch with you again brings back many memories. I hope you don't mind if I share some of them with you.

My memories start in the 2nd grade class we share. At some point during that year, I develop a crush on you. Whenever someone mentions your name or I see you, the butterflies rush into my tummy and I am entranced. You become the "rich girl in the mansion that I have the crush on" and I watch from a distance.

The distance isn't about how you treat me. You are always kind to me. The distance is about my insecurities and my perspective of being a poor kid who isn't in your league.

We go to different schools for the next three years. Then, in sixth grade, we are back in school together. Again, whenever someone mentions your name or I see you, the butterflies rush into my tummy and I am entranced. My perspective doesn't change. I stay on the fringe of your life, afraid to enter into it.

As we go through school, our paths cross many times. The butterflies always return. I always stay on the fringe.

Time goes by, we go our separate ways, move away from our hometown, marry, and live our lives.

Then, a few weeks ago, almost thirty years after my last contact with you, you send a friend request to me. Once I figure out the identity of The Crush, the butterflies return en masse. I am stunned.

During the past thirty years, my perspective has changed a great deal. I don't hide behind fears or insecurities. I know that my emotions are the voice of my soul and I'm learning to listen, really listen, to them. I decide to accept the friend request. I tell you that you made my day. Truthfully, you made my MONTH!

Then, with every little message, the butterflies flutter. This is a busy time of the year for me so I don't respond to them. I focus on my work.

However, when you post pictures recently, the butterflies turn into something larger, something grander, something I still can't describe, and something I can no longer ignore.

Looking back, my crush on you wasn't a physical or sexual attraction. It was a "soul cry" of some type, something I can't really explain. It wasn't logical or reasonable. However, it was real to me. Now, I realize it never left. It still isn't logical or reasonable. However, it is real to me so I have to respond.

The pictures show your spirit, your heart, your... I don't know how to put it into words but I see something in those pictures that is very special. I keep those pictures open in my browser all morning Friday and stare at them often; trying to figure out what it is about them, about you, that entrances me.

I don't know the answer...yet.

As I think about it over the weekend, I know that I have to tell you. If I have any doubts, they disappear *when, without prompting, my wife says, "You need to tell her. She needs to know."*

So, I have.

If we lived closer to one another, I'd suggest we meet for coffee or lunch so we could talk. We would catch up on the past and compare each other's journey. I suspect it wouldn't take long to figure out why I have this "soul cry" for you.

However, because of the distance, the best I can do at this point is to send you an email, describe my experiences, and see if you are open to starting a dialogue. I believe there is a significant reason that I have these feelings and it goes beyond a childhood crush. Perhaps you have something to teach me, I have something to teach you, or maybe it is something that will completely surprise both of us.

I look forward to hearing from you.

With great admiration,

Matthew

When I sent the email, I sensed a shift inside me. I walked away from the computer and released any attachment to the results. I discovered I was at peace.

Less than two hours later, I received a response. I opened it without hesitation.

The Crush was at a loss for words. She had no idea of my feelings. She insisted on calling me the next week.

I responded and she called the next day. In fact, we talked several times that week.

We caught up on our past. We shared spiritual stories. We laughed. We cried. A weight came off my shoulders as I realized that my intuition about her wasn't wrong. In fact, it was completely accurate.

The Crush and I had a great deal to offer one another. She taught a discipline that I just started learning. My writing confirmed her discoveries.

During our conversations, The Crush mentioned several books. One resonated with me. I knew I had to get it. I used the internet to put it on hold at the local library before we finished our conversation. I picked it up the next day and read it in one night.

I found everything else written by the author and put all of his books on hold. I read them. The Wife read them. Our children read them. Every book was jammed full of insight on following intuition.

Suddenly, I trusted everything coming from my intuition without a trace of doubt. I acted without hesitation. Everything in my life accelerated. It was easier to hear my intuition because I trusted it. I no longer blocked it.

My relationships experienced fulfillment because trusting my intuition was necessary before I could trust others. My businesses experienced remarkable profit during "down economic times" because I took massive action immediately instead of overanalyzing what my intuition was telling me.

I suddenly had the courage to close a profitable business because it distracted me from my passion of writing and coaching. I scheduled two weeks of training to help my sons with their business. Life became easy, so easy that I wondered each day what remarkable thing will come my way today.

Even though I wasn't aware of it, my unfulfilled childhood crush subconsciously hindered me from trusting my internal guidance. It prevented me from clearly hearing my source, my God. This happened because I thought it was wrong once. Truthfully, I just didn't have all the facts yet.

Learning to trust my intuition moved my life to a new level. I still wonder what remarkable thing will come my way today.

So the question I have today is "Is my intuition trustworthy today?" My dreams, my feelings, and everything else that I know to be my intuition say "yes." I think the key for me is to trust it and not be attached to it, not interpret it with my knowledge. I will be out and it will feel good. We will go to New York City to celebrate our anniversary, and it will be fun. It may not be our 25th anniversary, but we will do this!

When I realized that it is still possible for us to get out tomorrow, I stopped to think about The Wife. I believe it is important for her to develop spiritual practice in this situation. However, if she chooses not to do so, is it better for her to get to a breaking point or to experience relief? In the past, I may have chosen the breaking point answer. Today, I see the wisdom of mercy. It is an obvious decision to choose mercy over breaking, especially if she can't grow softly strong in her cracked places until the pressure of this situation has been reduced.

A person can choose to grow softly strong or grow strong with resistance. Growing while resisting just adds to the crack. It isn't fun. It creates stress, unhealthy stress. This is what The Wife experienced a few days ago when she had chest pains and her left arm when numb. They took her to medical to run an EKG and everything was OK physically. However, I am

138

concerned about the mental stress producing physical symptoms.

Sometime, people choose to respond to stress by behaving in a way that causes them to gain attention. Many times, this behavior creates a sickness, injury, or other event that garners sympathy. It is a cry for love. If the cry is answered in such a way that it relieves the stress, the individual will temporarily recover. The only way the individual can permanently recover is to recognize that it is not the external situation that caused the stress. It is the internal response to the external situation.

When I read the New Testament stories a couple weeks ago, I thought about angels leading me out of here. While it would have been a good story, I realize it would have resulted in more charges. So, instead, I asked the angels to mess up the indictment paperwork so it wouldn't be able to be used by 5 pm on the 23rd. I wonder...

The Monk told me a story yesterday about underwear. I gave up all our clothes upon entry including my boxers. This is typical of inmates placed into a psych POD. Then, we have to figure out how to replace them and take care of them. We may order undergarments, socks, and shoes from commissary. We may send laundry to be washed once a week. However, this really isn't often enough for most of people so each person develops a system that works for him.

For example, I noticed one guy wears briefs under his boxers under his MDC pants. Another guy wears boxers only and he rotates the pairs. This is where The Monk's story comes in. The past couple of mornings, he's noticed Sad Sack working on something in the sink during the early morning hours.

Apparently, he's soiling himself during the night and then washing his shorts in the sink. This is the same sink where inmates brush teeth and wash hands. I'm not sure what a better solution is for him but the whole situation makes me glad I'm not brushing my teeth over there.

Monday, December 27, 2010

This is my third Monday in jail. Looking back, the time has passed quickly so I am assuming future time will pass quickly too. I alternate between the desire to leave here and my practice of remaining in the moment. When I remind myself that this moment is all there is, time becomes irrelevant. I still have much to learn about this.

From my cell, I just heard The Monk talking to Head Counselor about Sad Sack's boxer washing in the hand wash and toothbrush sink. Head Counselor's advice was to "take it to circle." Circle is a technique that the POD uses to address questionable behavior. During Group, a mentor calls the offender into the circle and the two of them place their chairs into the middle of the circle. The mentor affirms the offender and then explains the issue. The offender can respond or he can ask for help resolving the situation. Head Counselor administers any needed discipline. I wasn't in Group today so I didn't get to see the results of the circle.

The noises here continue to amaze me. The toilets no longer sound like toilets to me. They sound like a forced air heater beginning to cycle. Then, they end with that conch shell sound that is more like the vibration that goes through some heating systems when the temperature changes.

The Screamer was in rare form last night. At times, it sounded like he was having a conversation with someone. It finally dawned on me that he may be a shaman who doesn't understand his gifts. There is significant evidence that those who speak, see, and hear the spirit realm are those people we certify as crazy.

The idea of "crazy people" being shamans resonates with me because if someone is constantly between two worlds and doesn't know it, that alters their view of reality. They live in this dimension and see the other one. When they talk about the other dimension, those of us in this dimension think they are crazy. The Monk says there is treatment and drugs to prevent people from hearing voices and seeing things so we don't have to do that. I have to wonder if these treatments hinder our culture from moving towards spirituality and love. Are we treating away the skills that are necessary for the next evolutionary step?

Obviously, there are skills needed to communicate spiritual realities effectively to a physical world. That is one of the things I do. That's why I write. That's why I teach. I want each side to be able to explain to the other side what they see and hear so each can see the other.

Am I a shaman? Not in the traditional definition. Do I see the spiritual realm? Absolutely. I talk with spirit. I chat with the subconscious mind of individuals alive today. I visit with great minds of the past. I pursue mastermind alliances that are greater than the sum of the individual participants.

These are techniques taught in Napoleon Hill's *Think and Grow Rich*. They are powerful in design and beautiful in application. I suspect that most of the people in this unit have connections to the spirit realm that they don't know what to do with. I may see if I can explore that with some of them today.

Starting today, I'm focusing on different areas of my body for the extra workouts. Today is crunches. I'll do 100 or more throughout the day. I'll do squats and pushups on other days. I can knock out 25 crunches or 15 pushups in a couple of minutes. If I do that several times throughout the day, I can easily meet my goals.

There is a suicide watch inmate across the POD from me. I suppose he isn't really suicidal because if he was, he'd have ample opportunity to kill himself. I say this because, more often than not, the rover on duty is asleep. I was standing at my door waiting for lunch to be served when I noticed this. I chuckled when the fire alarm went off and woke the rover. I wonder if that's why they don't fix the alarm.

I just had an interesting thought. Age fifty is so often the time when a man begins something new. I will be fifty in September. However, if I work back 9 months, my moment of conception would be now, give or take a few weeks. As I sit here, I sense a significant change taking place. Is it a relationship change? Is it a career change? Is it something else?

Of course, there will be change. Change is how the world works. We're always changing. To think otherwise is to deny reality so I suppose thinking about the details of the change doesn't matter. Still, there are obvious signposts in our lives that point to the significant, major changes and this appears to be one of those.

I can't get too caught up in what the change will be. I understand that I need the darkness of the future to apply faith and freedom to my life. I also understand there are indicators that prepare us for those changes so it is wise to recognize those indicators when they appear.

Monday, December 27, 2010 (PM)

It's official. I'm indicted and I assume The Wife is too. My indictment happened without any involvement on my part. The only way I learned about it was when a staff member came and escorted me to the fingerprint room. I was fingerprinted when I first arrived at MDC so I'm not sure why they had to fingerprint me again. Apparently, it has something to do with the case going from Metro Court to District Court.

It was explained to me like this. When I was arrested, they arraigned me in Metro Court. This was the hearing I had the day after I was arrested. Metro Court has ten business days to indict me. If they indict me, then the case goes to District Court and District Court has ten business days to arraign me. If that information is accurate, that means at least two more weeks here, maybe more. I'll need to give the kids some direction tomorrow regarding management of our financial affairs.

It seems strange to me that there could be a hearing in court, involving my case, and I would not be allowed to attend and my attorney would not be present. Everyone I talk to about this says, "Oh, that's just the way it is." Once again, this doesn't seem to be the America I learned about in school...

This POD continues to evolve. New guys come in, others go out. There are two Hispanic gentlemen that are a joy: Smiley and Stoic. Smiley is always smiling and encouraging others. Stoic is the man who lost his son. He and I look out for one another with the newspaper by making sure the other has read it.

Another new man, Worrier, came in a couple days ago. He is a large man who is nervous as can be about being in here.

The Drummer has become more insistent than The Vulture in trying to get food from other inmates. Between meals, he attempts to get food other inmates have purchased through commissary. At meals, he attempts to trade his entire meals for coffee.

Coffee is one of the addictive products available legally at MDC. MDC is a smoke free environment so there are no cigarettes. Of course, alcohol and illegal drugs are not allowed. Inmates can go to medical and have medications prescribed for them if they use legal drugs.

Because this is a psych POD, the only coffee allowed in here is decaf. It doesn't matter to these guys. They will trade entire meals for coffee. One guy even traded his reading glasses for coffee.

I had wondered about The Screamer's ability to comprehend conversation and maintain social skills. They let him out for dinner tonight so I observed his interactions with the other POD members. He was coherent and pleasant. I had looked in on him earlier today when he started screaming again. He was asleep, shaking in the bed, talking in his sleep. I'm almost certain he has the gifts of a shaman. I wonder if he knows what he is seeing or if he thinks he has a disease.

I'm not an expert on shamanism but I have studied it quite a bit. One of my sources is a movie and book called *The Horseboy*. It is the story of a father's search to bring healing to his autistic son. During his search, he discovers that his son behaves "normally" when he is around horses. He also discovers that a local shaman brings temporary relief to his son through a ceremony. With these two pieces of information, the father decides to take his son to the birthplace of horses and search for shamans that can bring healing.

The movie and book each document their adventures. More than once, the father wonders if he is the crazy one as they trek through wilderness areas in pursuit of healing. In the end, the father discovers that the "disease" called "autism" is the special wiring the brain needs for an individual to practice successfully as a shaman.

As I read the book and viewed the movie, I was struck by how often our society judges and sets aside those things that seem abnormal to us. We become afraid of those things we don't understand and we lock them away, not understanding that we are locking away potential solutions to our largest problems.

An autistic person's obsessive behavior is nothing more than a remarkable ability to concentrate on one given task. This skill doesn't fit within our multitasking society. However, it is the very skill needed to solve our world's toughest problems. It is the very skill needed to show us how to bridge the physical and spiritual worlds so that we can live peacefully with one another.

I did 110 crunches today along with my usual TFT workout. I can't see myself in a mirror so I don't know how my body looks. (The mirrors at MCC are tiny pieces of shiny metal that only give me a one foot square skewed reflection of my face.) Of course, the body's appearance is constantly changing so it is only a small indicator of how a person feels. I decided several months ago to use other factors to determine if I'm eating, exercising, and resting enough. That has worked for me and I've felt good since that time.

I've noticed that when I'm on a diet or trying to accomplish certain physical goals, I feel deprived. This feeling causes an attitude of scarcity and crimps the abundance that I know is naturally mine. In addition, a deprived feeling is not a healthy feeling because it is usually accompanied by feeling weak. I know when I feel strong, I feel healthy so I changed my focus from maintaining a weight to maintain a feeling of strength.

Now that I have additional time, I am determined to use it to make me stronger on all levels – especially on the level of love.

I think that's my biggest challenge in here. How do I love? The challenge is big because there are so many things to hate: the barbaric act of caging humans, the slowness of the legal system, the ineptness of the staff, the attitude of those who judge inmates. When I realize that one act, classified as illegal, that takes place in a few minutes, can so drastically take so much time from a person, I'm appalled. Sometimes, these are simply mistakes, easily corrected. However, because of the system, correction isn't possible. I hate this. It provides many opportunities to criticize or complain.

I now get a sense of what other people go through and how difficult it can be to "keep the faith" when things aren't as you want them to be. I yearn to love in the midst of this system I hate. And, I know I cannot love and hate at the same time. It is impossible. Therefore, if I am to love, I must embrace this system, love it, be grateful for the opportunity to write, read, meditate, and contemplate so I can learn how to love all, even the painful parts, so I can embrace and change them.

I know that I cannot change the things I resist because what I resist persists. Hating the system only empowers it. I know that my emotional energy is better spent on emotions other than hate, so I will love. I will take the energy that I feel when the hate is there and neutralize it. I will keep the energy, while removing the hate filter. I will then take that energy and use it for love and gratefulness.

One of my fears today was that I would be moved out of this POD. I noticed every move slip that has been delivered to the CO today and I prayed they wouldn't call my name. PAC 2 Psychiatrist even came up to me today and said they were going day to day with me and ultimately it would be up to security (the COs). I think I may be secure in here for a while. They just moved a couple of guys, including Stoic, so there is ample room for new guys. I'm grateful.

I think part of my purpose here is to learn to identify with those in this situation. It s a lesson in compassion. I see several benefits. 1) I will be more skilled in coaching; 2) My experience will give me greater credibility; 3) My challenges will make me more real to others because they will know what I have been through.

149

Tuesday, December 28, 2010

I was served jelly with breakfast this morning. That was a first. Since Saturday, we've had granola bars instead of cookies at lunch. That's a nice improvement too. I've heard rumors that there is new management coming into MDC, so I wonder if the menu changes are the result of the new management.

Last night, just before bed, I found myself feeling "at home" here. I shook myself out of it and started to go into fear again when I stopped and said, "No, It's OK to be at home wherever I am." That's the goal isn't it? To be content in all situations. To be at peace. To be free.

Pema Chodron says that when we sit with our pain, our suffering, we allow ourselves to crack, to soften. Out of that crack comes compassion, what she calls *BODHICHITTA*. What cracks in that process is the wals of anger, separation, and fear that we've built into our lives so that we don't have to face reality. This suffering, this pain, is not to be feared but embraced so we can allow the love to fill the crack. It's another way we grow softly strong in the cracked places.

Buddhist teachings are about peace. However, they teach a warrior's mentality. The two ideas (or at least the terms used for those ideas) are opposites: Peace and War. I understand they are saying we must be aware, alert, and disciplined, like a warrior, to practice peace. Still the term "warrior" bothers me. What would be a better term? What would communicate the intense pursuit of peace in a state of constant, conscious awareness?

One of the noises I haven't yet written about comes from the sink drains. They are often quiet. However, when they make sounds, the result is astounding. They often play a complex rhythmic beat that goes on for hours and hours. Sometimes, the sound resembles an African jungle rhythm. Other times, it is a steady rock beat. I suppose the size of the pipes and distance of the dropping water makes the sound. It is quite fascinating to hear and to use as a sound for sleep induction.

Yesterday, I feared being moved from this POD. Then, I decided I wouldn't be moved for a while. My intuition was preparing me for what actually happened today. I went from PAC 2, home of about 25 mostly calm inmates to SEG 1, a POD of the same size that is the home of more than 90 inmates.

My heart sank when I was told I was being moved to a segregation POD. I had heard that meant I would be in a cell with at least one and possibly two other inmates for 23 hours a day. Therefore, I was surprised when I walked into SEG 1 and saw everyone out of their cells. The CO told me to sit at a table until they figured out which cell to put me in.

I held my two blankets, my two notepads, my two ink pens, and a small bag of toiletry items while I looked around my new home. I noticed than many of the inmates were older than me. In PAC 2, I was the 2nd or 3rd oldest. Here, about a third of the guys were older than me. I watched carefully to see if there was a pecking order. There didn't seem to be. About twenty inmates were watching TV. Another thirty or so were scattered around the tables; playing cards, chess, and dominoes. I could see about a dozen inmates outside watching other inmates play handball. The atmosphere felt like summer camp. The inmates were laughing, talking, and enjoying themselves. The noise resonated within the POD creating a loud hum.

SEG 1 was about the same size as PAC 2. However, the layout was different. From the sally port, the commons area expanded into a large trapezoid. The TV hung over meeting rooms along the right wall in the narrowest part of the POD. The space expanded into a large commons area with tables on the left and the CO station on the right. Behind the CO station was a wall of windows and behind the windows was the outdoor recreational area. The wall on the left side contained two levels of cells. It adjoined the fourth wall with more cells. A metal staircase came down from the upper level, starting at the corner of those two walls and ending in the middle of commons area below, directly across from the CO's station. I noticed showers on both levels, at the top of the stairs and underneath the staircase.

The upper level was nothing more than the cells, showers, and a hallway. The hallway had a series of horizontal and vertical purple bars on the interior. The bars were far enough apart to allow clear views and close enough together to keep someone from slipping between them.

A couple of inmates came up and introduced themselves. I noticed that several spoke to one another in Spanish. I wasn't sure if they only spoke Spanish or if they had already figured out I didn't speak it and they were talking about me.

The CO assigned me to Cell 29: on the upper level. I made my way up the stairs and noticed an inmate hanging out, leaning against the bars. I asked him if 29 was his cell and he said it was. I introduced myself to him and explained that I was his new cell mate. Cellmate One visibly winced.

He then went and got me a "boat" which was a plastic platform, about eight inches tall. It was hollow underneath and it was almost large enough to hold one of those three inch thick mattresses used at MDC. Looking in from the door, there was a bunk bed on the left side of the cell. The stainless steel toilet and sink combo was on the wall opposite the door. To the right of the toilet and sink, was a desk. The layout was similar to my room in PAC 2 except everything was reversed.

Since Cellmate One and Cellmate Two already had their stuff on the desks and bed, I realized the small space on the floor between the bed and wall would be my living space. It was about 21 square feet.

I stepped outside as a couple of other inmates helped Cellmate One put the boat into the cell and threw the mattress on top of it. The CO had told me earlier that he would get me a bedroll before lockdown. Now, Cellmate One and the other inmates asked me if I had it. I told them I didn't and they told me to ask the CO again because he would forget.

I learned that SEG 1 didn't have mentors. It had BOs. "BO" stood for "Bay Orderly." I had learned earlier that MDC used naval terms. Therefore, the doors were called "sally ports." The guards were called "Commanding Officers" (COs), and the inmates who helped keep the POD clear were called "BOs." Once I heard the term in SEG 1, I remembered that the mentors were sometimes called BOs in PAC 2.

I learned that the BOs received a small commissary stipend each month for their work. The value was about $15 or fifty cents a day. These guys served meals, cleaned the commons area, and handled anything else that wasn't in the staff's job description. Of course, I realized they weren't doing it for the money. Since they had to clean when everyone else was in their cells, the BOs had more freedom than everyone else. In addition, they had access to extra meal trays and anything else that arrived in the POD. Therefore, they had power because they controlled who received them.

Two of the BOs finished helping Cellmate One, warily introduced themselves, and welcomed me to the POD. After they left, Cellmate One filled me in on the rules for "his cell." He said he liked to keep it clean. He told me to spit in the toilet when I brushed my teeth so that the drain wouldn't stink. He explained that we would always warn one another before flushing so that we wouldn't be surprised by the sudden loud noise.

He told me that he and Cellmate Two didn't bother each other. Cellmate Two had a girlfriend that he wrote letters to every day and he kept to himself. I explained that I was a neat freak, that I didn't need much space, and that I was writing a book so I wouldn't bother him. He seemed relieved at that but I could tell he wasn't comfortable with having a new guy in the cell.

Cellmate Two came into the room and introduced himself. I apologized for taking up their space. Cellmate Two laughed and said it wasn't my fault. He was sure I didn't want to be there. I liked him immediately.

The CO called my name and I went downstairs to his station. He delivered the promised bedroll and I went back upstairs to make my bed. For the first time since my arrival at MDC, I had sheets, two of them. I wrapped one around the mattress for a cover, and tucked the edges of the other one, along with one of my blankets under the sides of the mattress. I left the other blanket folded. I would continue to use it as my pillow.

I stuffed my toiletries and writing materials between the boat and the wall and decided to go downstairs to see if I could become comfortable in my new environment. Truthfully, I was scared. I knew nothing about the people in this POD. Were they violent? Did they initiate new people? I pushed aside those questions and decided to see this as an adventure. The way to approach something new as an adventure is to be more curious than afraid.

I noticed two inmates playing chess. One was The Competitor, an inmate I played handball with in PAC 2 during day one of my incarceration. He had been in PAC 2 for about a week and we had played a game of chess there. I didn't play well and he won easily. I sat down at a table, said "hi" to The Competitor and watched. Immediately, The Competitor began to talk about how good a player I was. I watched as he used me to trash-talk to the other guy.

The other guy didn't seem to mind. I wondered why The Competitor would do this. The only reason I could determine was that he wanted to elevate his status in the POD. In addition, I suspected The Competitor sensed my unease at being in a new place and he wanted to help. He could praise me by trash-talking to his opponent. I recognized the compassion in his act and it brought me comfort.

The game ended and it was time for lockdown. I went to my cell and thought about the change. Even though this was a segregation pod, apparently, I could be out of my cell more. This was a relief because I wasn't looking forward to sharing a small cell with two other people. I wasn't comfortable yet but it was a start.

After lockdown, I went downstairs and waited for dinner. Several guys introduced themselves to me and asked if I had just got there or if I was a transfer from another POD. I watched chess games and chatted about POD safety. Everyone told me this was a safe POD and there was no one in there that I needed to be concerned about.

I talked to Daughter One today and learned a few things. She said one of my clients wanted to raise money for our legal defense. I'm grateful. She also said that My Helper is thinking about running my business until this is resolved.

We met My Helper several years ago. Son Two's ex-girlfriend and her mom both worked for My Helper at her tax shop. My Helper had prepared taxes for more than twenty years and she was tired of being the business owner. She came to me more than a year ago and offered me her clients because she was closing her shop and moving to Florida. We negotiated a deal and I was preparing for my business to triple in 2011.

She was visiting New Mexico for the holidays and I had told Daughter Two to ask her if she wanted to run my business until I got out. I didn't think she would because she had told me she hated New Mexico in the winter. However, she was at least thinking about it. I wondered how that would evolve.

There are almost 90 inmates in this POD, all in about the same space as 25 guys in the other POD. I'm amazed at how we warehouse people in this system. My goal is to embrace and change our world but how can you do that when you see the barbaric methods used. Imagine having three guys in a room and then, the toilet overflows. That isn't happening in my cell but it is happening just down the hall as I write. The overflowing toilets are on the top floor so the water is running out the door and over the balcony onto the first floor. This was the second toilet to do this today. The BOs have been busy mopping, moving trashcans to catch the water, and keeping the place clean.

I have discovered there is no newspaper in here unless I borrow it from the guys who get the paper mailed to them. There are books to read so I can continue my practice of reading and writing. I can see that the time will go by quicker in here than the other POD because I have less time to be by myself.

Wednesday, December 29, 2010

I received more insight today about why this segregation POD runs like a general population (GP) POD when the POD's new Captain arrived on the floor this morning and addressed us. He says he hates segregation PODs and that is why he runs this one as a GP POD. I'm grateful – that's for sure. He seems fair. He explained his "rules" and they are reasonable.

He told us that he had no obligation to give us soap or any hygiene supplies other than a towel and toilet paper. I had been told otherwise upon my arrival at MDC so this was a surprise to me. I knew I had a little money in my commissary account, so I decided to purchase soap and a toothbrush this week. I had enough toothpaste to last until the following week and I decided to ask the kids to put a little more money into my account.

I couldn't figure out how to do TFT today so I was in a funk for a while. There simply isn't enough room in the cell. Finally, I went downstairs and circled the pod 21 times in lieu of doing the spinning. Then, I came back to my bunk for the 21 leg lifts and went outside for the last three rites. We'll see how that works tomorrow. It's supposed to snow.

The more I talk with Cellmate Two, the more I like him. He is a sports fan, lives in Edgewood, and has used My Attorney as an attorney. He is in here or parole violation because his ex-girlfriend filed charges. It's another case of someone trying to ruin someone's life by making a phone call. The judicial/law enforcement system arrests first and takes part of a person's life before they go through the hearing process. I understand it and the more I see it, the less I agree with it.

Cellmate One is a repeat offender. He's been booked into MDC 21 times. He's restless and doesn't have great social skills. On the pro side, he's neat and clean. When he's talking, he picks a cuss word and uses it as a noun, verb, adjective, and adverb. It's pretty funny. He's loud too. He has to know what's going on throughout the POD so he's always yelling and making some other kind of noise after we are locked down.

I keep telling myself I've learned what I need to learn and it's time to get out of here. In life, at least in my life, I've encountered problems, worked on them, and let the miracles happen. Things work out and life goes on. That is universal. However, that doesn't seem to work in here. There is nothing to work on in here, just time to kill

OK, that isn't totally true. There are things to work on but I can't work on getting out of here or at least getting out of here quickly and that's my heart cry right now. I've done everything I know to do with that, so the next thing is to find what else I can work on

I suppose that is to find better ways to kill time or maybe spend time. What is that? Meditation, other spiritual practices, reading, reaching out to others? Surviving?

One way we spend time in here is through "command call." This is the practice of standing outside our cells, hands behind our back, when an officer comes on the floor, when the medical staff dispenses medicine, or when it's time for chow.

Each command call event requires a minimum of ten minutes and sometimes last as long as thirty.

Last night, my cell mates were reading old newspapers, including the one from December 9th, the day after our arrest. I saw the front page headline, above the fold, that said, "Couple Accused of Molesting Children " I didn't read the article and didn't comment. I just kept reading my book.

I was writing earlier today about miracles. I was down, frustrated because I live a life of miracles and I don't feel like I'm seeing them here. I have to remember that to see miracles, I must have miracle eyes. I opened my eyes and found a miracle today. A fellow inmate, Religious Guy, told me about his situation. He had two life terms plus 18 years hanging over his head. After two years of negotiations, he prayed on a Monday and asked for an answer by Friday. On that Friday, his attorney surprised him by coming to visit and telling him they had dropped everything to a four year sentence and he only had one more year since they'd given him a 75% rule. That's the kind of miracle I'm talking about.

I played some chess yesterday and played cards today. The deck of cards we played with was old, faded, and soft. In fact, I'd never seen such a flimsy deck of cards. It's all we have, so it's what we use. I somehow feel guilty playing cards when there is so much I could be doing if I wasn't in here. However, I can't do that while in here so I work at relaxing into what I can do and not fretting about what I can't control.

I remember the guy who wrote *Four Hour Work Week* realized his business life would go on without him when he stepped away from it. Not only did his business survive without him. It flourished. I'm learning that too. When I move from one place, I leave a void for other people to fill. They grow and mature more through my absence than through my presence.

The guys in this POD are friendly. They want to talk. They want to reach out to people. One older gentleman sits in the commons area and plays solitaire until enough guys show up to play Rummy. Fighter Pilot is a kind, grandfatherly type. He started flying as a teenager and he claims to hold the record for the most fighter pilot missions flown in a year in Vietnam. He threw me a piece of candy today, just to be nice. I heard another inmate talking about how someone bought him coffee in his commissary order. Little things like that bring out deep emotions in these guys. The receiver of the coffee cried when he told the story about the coffee.

Going to the bathroom when there are three guys sharing a toilet has a certain dance to it. Peeing is simple. Some guys keep the water in the sink running while they go. I suppose that serve two purposes. It helps them go and it covers up the sound of their own tinkling. Shitting is more complex. Cellmate One set the example today. He went into the cell during a command call, put up a sheet over the end of the bed for privacy, and did his business. We all respect each other and understand it is just part of the circumstances.

Showering in this POD is similar to the other POD with a few differences. For one, we get to keep our towels for a week so there is no rush to grab a towel, take a shower, and turn it in by 12:30. For another, there are eight showers, instead of six. There are four upstairs and four downstairs. Each shower area has two showers on each side. A small half wall juts out in front of each shower area providing token privacy. I say token because anyone within the commons area can easily see into the showers.

The unwritten rule is that it is OK to take a shower on an empty side but not to join someone who is already taking a shower on one side. Some guys shower daily. Some shower twice a day. Some don't shower unless the complaints about their odor force them to do so. When those people shower, their cell mates often applaud.

Taking a shower is also a way to wash undergarments. Many of the inmates strip to their shorts and shower without removing them. Or, if they do remove them, it is at the end of their shower when they wash the garments. I'm not sure if showering in shorts is a modesty issue or just a convenient way to do laundry. I suspect it is a little of both.

Thursday, December 30, 2010

I can understand why some inmates would be afraid of showering. It goes back to the fear each of us felt the first time we were asked to take a shower in our high school gym class. I remember thinking, "You mean you want me to shower in front of my classmates?" That experience was supposed to help us prepare for life by becoming comfortable with our bodies. I wonder if students are still forced to group shower as part of the physical education process. If not, I wonder what philosophy changed.

In addition, some of the inmates may be frightened to shower in here because this POD is the so-called "perv pod." It houses inmates facing sexual charges. In most cases, those charges are not violent and that is why none of us have to worry too much about violence in here. I've learned that the inmates actually signed wavers when they changed this segregation POD to function as a GP POD.

Of course, since this is a SEG POD, the simplest task becomes a reason for lockdown. If we change sheets, uniforms, and towels, we must go into lockdown. If it is time for commissary delivery, we must go into lockdown. If it is time for chow or medications, we go to command call, which is an abbreviated lockdown where we must stand outside the doors of our cells. If an officer comes into the POD, we must go into command call.

After several weeks of telling myself this situation is for my benefit, I'm actually starting to feel that way. My Helper has decided to stay in New Mexico and take care of my tax business while I'm in here. I don't know exactly how this will work out but I'm thrilled about it.

Daughter One said that The Wife has mailed me a letter. I'm glad. It will be good to hear from her. In addition, I'm relieved that she is processing this situation in a positive manner. Today was supposed to be the day we left for New York City to celebrate our 25th wedding anniversary.

Daughter One also said that we have received numerous letters from friends and clients proclaiming our character and supporting us. These can be used in court to help us be released. She is passing them on to Substitute Attorney.

I'm currently reading *Plain Speaking, an Oral Biography of Harry S. Truman*. According to the book, Truman didn't use advertising men. Instead, he spoke the truth, didn't hide anything, and let the people decide for themselves. It sounds familiar to me. Open, naked communication is what people respond to and it is what people want and need. Would it work today? I'm sure it would. The challenge would be how to do that within the parameters of today's media.

Today's media doesn't report the news. It creates stories based on actual events. This makes it difficult, almost impossible, for the truth to be told through the media. I've heard many things about my current situation that were reported through the media that have no factual basis at all. Of course, those stories are portrayed as truth and since many people think the news is factual, they believe they are true.

It would take guts to campaign today the way Truman did. He wouldn't cooperate with the Democratic National Convention, so he didn't have access to their money. In addition, he wouldn't take huge contributions because he didn't want to have to answer to the contributors. I'm not sure he could become president in today's system. However, I'm sure people would respond favorably to him if given the opportunity.

Truman liked Sir Francis Bacon's quote: "The good things which belong to prosperity are to be wished but the good things that belong to adversity are to be admired." I like it too. There are good things coming from my adversity and that means there will be admiration. That means it will bring attention to my message of peace, love, and openness. Even in here, I feel the responsibility of that message and my mind is racing with ideas on how to share that.

Some new guys came into the POD today. Immediately, a gentleman I was playing cards with wanted me to be his 3rd cell mate so he wouldn't have to have one of the new guys in his cell. It worked out OK without me making the move because none of the new guys were assigned to his cell.

That experience reminded me that fear hits everyone in here. In fact, each man's emotional capacity is almost at full because he doesn't know when he will be released. As long as that man stays busy and is not disrupted by a change, he is OK. However, if something odd happens, the emotional and mental meltdowns start.

Extra noise, new inmates, and unscheduled activities are all capable of starting the complaining. One technique the COs use that currently causes the most complaining is locking our cell doors when we're not in lockdown. I can't go into the cell if I'm out of it and I can't come out of the cell if I'm in it. That makes it a challenge to use the toilet and take a shower. I'm not sure why they do that. The inmates think the staff just wants to "fuck with us."

Another source of complaint is the phone situation. There are five phones and only one of them is usable. There are ninety inmates trying to use one usable phone. WOW...

I have always been different from those people around me and that is true of my experience at MDC. Some of the inmates purposely make decisions to be incarcerated. They talk about the illegal activities they want to do upon release, so they can return. The staff does an adequate job but not a thorough one. They do enough to get by and get a check. It seems that the goal for each person is just to kill time so he can do something else.

I'm struggling with this. I always desire to do more, contribute more, help more. I continue to read, write, and workout. However, I know that part of my experience includes investing in my fellow inmates. To do that, I must spend time with them. I've decided to do that by playing cards and sharing stories.

Light and Liberty came in today and led a Bible Study. When invited to attend, I passed. The Beard, one of the guys at our table, asked me why I didn't attend because he thought I was a spiritual person.

"I went to church and Bible study for more than thirty-five years and I don't usually participate now. In fact, the leaders usually don't want me to attend because I ask questions they don't want to answer. I appreciate what religion did for me because it laid a foundation for what I believe now. However, I've found it is in everyone's best interest if I don't participate."

"It sounds like you spent all that time in religion and ended up with a certificate in cynicism."

I smiled and thought about what he said. "I suppose that's accurate, I am cynical of religion – especially when it doesn't do what it says it is going to do."

"I understand."

His response came without a smile. I sensed that he too had been disappointed by a religion that didn't keep promises.

I have wondered if the crow would keep me company in SEG 1 like it did in PAC 2. I received my answer today. I briefly went outside to do TFT. I only did one set outside because of the weather. A winter storm was coming into the area and the wind was horrendous. In spite of this the cold weather, wind, and brief time outside, a crow flew overhead. I welcomed the reassurance.

Speaking of reassurance, I've noticed that, even when incarcerated, human beings need touch from other human beings. Without it, health isn't possible. Studies done with orphaned babies demonstrate that when the babies are not held on a daily basis, the babies develop significant physiological issues that threaten their survival. If the anger and violence within our society is any indication, adults who are not held on a daily basis also develop significant physiological issues that threaten their survival.

Touch must be subtle in MDC because no one wants to bother anyone or be accused of making sexual advances. Even with these obstacles, I've noticed that touch occurs. Sometimes it's only a poke, a bump, or a pat on the back, but it happens.

Surprisingly, several inmates greet me with a handshake each day. Other inmates use the street greeting of a handshake combined with a hug. Human beings must physically connect with one another and will do so in spite of the circumstances.

I've also noticed that if peaceful touch can't take place, the touch may become violent. When a person is constantly rejected by other people, he lashes out because of the lack of love. In an effort to have this need met, he may create a violent situation so he can fight (touch) other people. Every time a fight almost happened in PAC 2, one of the participants was someone the POD had rejected.

Tonight was the delivery of commissary. Yesterday, I ordered some toiletry items, so I was expecting them to call my name as they passed out the orders. I didn't expect them to call it twice. I had just put my first order away when I heard my name again.

I stuck my head out the door and asked the BO in charge if he called my name.

"Yes, you have an internet order."

I had heard that people on the outside could order items for me but never considered that would happen. I went down the stairs and discovered a massive commissary order. I barely knew how to respond. I looked at the packing slip for the order and saw that College Friend was the giver. My emotions churned within me as I compared the items in the bag with the items on the sheet.

I had purposely stayed away from the commissary goodies. I didn't want to be too comfortable in jail. After my first few days in jail, I had released all my possessions except for my writing tablets and ink pens. I wasn't sure I wanted to have

170

to deal with possessions. A lot of stuff meant I was going to be in one place for a while. I wanted jail to be a transient experience, almost uncomfortable. I didn't want any of the comforts of home.

I carried the bag to my cell, placed it under my boat, sat on my bunk, and cried. I was surprised at my response. There were numerous items that I needed, including toothpaste, socks, undergarments, writing tablets, pre-stamped envelopes, and ink pens. In addition, there were things I wanted like snacks and candy. I realized that even good things could be a source of emotional turmoil when a person's emotional capacity is full.

As I processed my experience, my emotions stabilized and I shifted into gratefulness. I felt the love of College Friend's gift and the tears continued to flow. I wanted to sob, to shake, so that my body could completely feel the emotions. However, this was jail and I had new cellmates and I didn't feel free enough to do this. I processed gently while I wrote my thoughts.

My cellmates sensed my emotion and carefully reached out to me. They had their own bounty from commissary and the new possessions had lightened their mood. Within moments after the completion of commissary delivery, our cell turned into a night at summer camp or a college dormitory. We stayed up late, eating goodies and playing dominoes. I realized I had spent most of the day playing games. Rummy in the afternoon, spades in the evening, and dominoes at night.

I reasoned that if I have to be in jail, I can at least make it fun. In some ways, it's like camping. I don't choose camping trips but when we go, I want it to be fun. Sleeping on my boat on the floor makes it feel even more like camping.

The ventilation system blows on me all night. It isn't a strong breeze, just a flow. It is cool air, just enough to keep me from being too warm. I may come up with a plan to divert it just enough so it isn't blowing right on me. It's a little thing really, but as I said earlier, little things grow to huge sizes when there is so little to do.

Part of College Friend's gift was a bunch of envelopes so I need to write letters. As I went to sleep, I realized her gift was perfect. It caused me to wonder if she has experienced a friend or relative being in jail before. I wonder if maybe she has been in jail. Her response to my situation has been quick, immediate, and perfect.

Friday, December 31, 2010

This morning, I can look out from my cell's open door on the orange clad group of men in the commons area. Some are watching TV, some are playing dominoes, others are playing cards, and a few are playing handmade board games like chess and Dungeons & Dragons. The rest are just hanging out, waiting, waiting for what's next. In some ways, it's like a huge barber shop or ma & pa restaurant where men go to while away the day away with idle chatter. I realize that for most of these men, this isn't that much different from their everyday lives on the outside. The only difference is that we can't leave here.

It is the final day of 2010. I don't really know what to think or how to feel about being here now. The date on the calendar is only a tic mark for time served when you're behind bars. I can look back at 2010 and see great accomplishments: A second grandbaby, growing businesses, our service to a local Chamber of Commerce, including bringing them to a point of financial break-even. There were the issues with Son One's Partner and House Guest. However, we walked through them and I think we did a good job with everything.

Then, there was the series of events that landed The Wife and me in jail, on the front page of the paper, and on TV. I have no idea what will happen in 2011. I know what I will work on when I get out of here. The question is "Will I get out?" and if so, "When?" For the first time in my life, I can't plan or schedule

173

or direct. I CAN ONLY LIVE THIS MOMENT, THIS INSTANT, AND DO NOTHING ELSE.

Of course, that's the way life is on the outside too. We can plan, schedule, and direct but things happen, life explodes and the universe orchestrates its "Conspiracy for Me." So, here I am, at the end of 2010 living the middle of this chapter, with no clue about the end and that's not so different from everyone else. We're all having experiences that allow us to grow softly strong in the cracked places.

One of the gentlemen in here is Religious Guy, the son of a famous country western singer. As a kid, I had one of his father's songs on a 45 or maybe on a County and Western Greatest Hits album. Religious Guy is a decent card player and he's been one of our spades players the past couple of nights. He's a nice enough guy who is really tied into Christianity and therefore, is often in a glum mood. He is grateful for his "Lord and Savior, Jesus Christ" and he feels badly that he has sinned so often.

I find it interesting that, even though each person comes to spirituality of his own accord, he feels a need to convert other people to that way of thinking. Even if another person or religion was instrumental in answering questions or explaining beliefs, each person makes an individual decision about spirituality only when those answers and beliefs resonate within his heart. There is nothing one person can do to convert another. It is only when an individual connects with the divine internally that something deeply significant takes place.

We had an interesting discussion in our cell during today's lockdown. Cellmate One said he is only afraid of one thing and that one thing is God. We asked him why and he said,

"He just was." Cellmate Two asked him if he was afraid of Hell and he said he didn't look that far ahead. He sighed and it was obvious he didn't want to talk about it anymore.

I thought about Cellmate One's obsession with cleaning and I suspected his obsessive-compulsive behavior was driven by a fear of God. He has a fear that he will do something wrong or leave something dirty, so he obsessively overcompensates for his fear. That explains why he dries the sink after every use. That explains why he wants the room so neat.

In addition, that would explain why someone with Cellmate One's obsessions would be arrested more than twenty times. My observation is that when people obsess about little things, they miss the big things. I have noticed that when someone has something in his life that can be corrected, he often spends time complaining about the other issues in his life.

I've thought a lot the past couple days about Head Counselor's questions to me while I was in PAC 2. He had just finished reading Scott Peck's *People of the Lie* and he was debating the existence of a psychological diagnosis of evil. I read the book a few years ago and decided then that evil was Peck's opinion. Peck had some dark experiences with clients, so he labeled them "evil." My observation was that he didn't have the skill set to work with them and needed a label to justify his failure. Evil is something the church and society accepts as truth, so it was convenient for Peck to use the concept for his book.

Head Counselor, as a counselor in jail, is struggling with his success rates. He believes he has failed in his task. When someone fails, there are two choices. One is to discover the source of the failure and take responsibility for it by initiating change. The other is to blame other people through name calling. Inmates call the judicial system "unfair." Free people, who have never been in jail, call inmates "criminals." Counselors and psychiatrists, who do not succeed with patients, label those patients with a medical diagnostic term that causes both the doctor and the patient to feel better about the challenge because it now has a name. Head Counselor, like Peck, was considering whether it was OK to make "evil" one of those diagnostic terms.

The problem with this technique of name calling is that is doesn't solve the problem and it doesn't improve the situation. It only gives everyone an excuse for the failure. The label, if accurate, may provide a potential plan for treatment based on previous situations where this label was used. However, if the label is inaccurate, the treatment plan won't work and, rather than reconsider the label, there is usually a tendency to stick with the misdiagnosis rather than admit a possible need to correct something else. Apparently, the need for those in control to be "right" is more important than the need of the individual to find what works.

As I looked around the POD today, I watched my fellow inmates watching TV, cheering during a football game, laughing during *America's Funniest Home Videos*. I watched them serve chow, give haircuts, clean the POD, and share candy with one another. I watched one inmate use the shiny, colorful wrappers from granola bars to make necklaces. I watched one transform potato chips bags into a sacred heart sculpture.

I found myself asking, "Are these people evil?" In my heart, the answer is "no." Each person has been accused of breaking the law so each of us is placed in a "secure environment" and labeled "an offender," "a criminal," "an inmate."

Of course, I observe behavior in here that shows social dysfunction. We were playing cards today and two dark skinned inmates were sitting on the steps, progressively talking louder. Fighter Pilot looked at them, looked at me, and said "Niggers." I hadn't heard that word used in a long time. I also overheard conversations with people talking about their next fight, next high, or next act of revenge.

Does the use of the word "nigger" make Fighter Pilot evil? Does the discussion of the next destructive act make a person evil?

A few hours after using the "N-word," Fighter Pilot brought out the chips he had saved from numerous lunches and served us nachos with bean dip for our New Year's Eve snack. He had planned this kind act for the people at his card table for several days. Every time I join this 74-year-old at his table, he always has a kind heart and inviting conversation. Is Fighter Pilot evil? Not in my opinion. He was frustrated with a behavior and name-called someone based on that.

Throughout the holiday season, I've noticed the same inmates who can't wait to fight, get high, or take revenge, give gifts from their commissary orders. They are encouraging other inmates when those inmates are down and discouraged.

Is it appropriate to label those people "evil?" The reader will have to make that judgment. My opinion is that every act is an act of love or a cry for love. It only takes one weak light bulb to illuminate the darkness.

Once someone is labeled, this label sticks with a person. We create labels like "evil" so that one group of people can control another through corrections. We create labels of "medical diagnosis" so that one group of people can control another through medication. We create the label of "sin" so that one group of people can control another group through religion.

We accept these labels as accurate when, in fact, humans are spiritual beings having a physical experience. These experiences don't define who we are. Who we are is established. We are God's children, with God's character, learning how to love.

Humans are not evil. Humans are not sick. Humans are not sinners. Humans are not good. Evil, sick, sin, and good are about perspective and opinion. That is all. They are not truth.

As I ate lunch today, I noticed the crow again. It flew over, circled back to my line of sight, and hovered. When I looked up, it dipped its' wings in acknowledgement and flew away.

I have had trouble with meditation since being moved into this POD. Having cellmates, being in a POD with ninety additional people, and the extra noise disrupts my time. Today, I remembered a meditation exercise that helped. I visualize myself as a mountain with people climbing on it, talking, making noise, playing their music, and doing whatever people do on a mountain. No matter what other people do, the mountain is still the mountain. If I visualize myself as that mountain, I can observe that the outside noise doesn't change who I am. This observation process allows me to maintain my meditation. Command Call is the perfect time to practice this. This gives me four times a day to meditate: the twice a day med distribution, immediately before lunch, and immediately before dinner.

Saturday, January 1, 2011

I am spending New Year's Day, my 25th Wedding Anniversary in jail. My emotions are on the edge of breaking. I've prepared for today twice. The first preparation was a celebration in New York City; a culmination of 25 years in a relationship with a successful family. We worked together, played together, learned together. We made agreements, changed them when they didn't work, set and accomplished goals. Today was to be a day to recognize how far we had come together.

Instead, it represents something else. I'm in jail. The Wife is in jail. We are charged with a combined 89 charges of harming our family. The irony of the situation would be funny if I didn't feel so sad. I won't see three of our children until the case is resolved. That will take months, possibly more than a year. Our oldest son has moved halfway across the country. The other four children are doing everything they know to do to keep things together with our home and businesses.

I'm contemplating instead of celebrating. When I realized the celebration wouldn't happen today, I went into survival mode so my emotions wouldn't overwhelm me. This was my second preparation. I prepared to be busy and get through the day quickly. I'm grateful that I slept well last night and slept extra this morning because that leaves less time to be awake today.

I awoke this morning to discover we're in lockdown because the facility is short-staffed. And, we're locked down for the entire day shift. That means no phone calls today and probably no visits either. Fortunately, I picked up several books from the library yesterday so I have stuff to read and I have a couple of letters to write

Cellmate One has decided to ignore me today. Maybe he has picked up on my mood. Maybe yesterday's conversation about God made him nervous. His obsessive and compulsive personality causes him to worry about everything. He reminds me of my mother.

He has spent most of the day playing chess with Cellmate Two and soundly beating him, alternating between trash talking and teaching Cellmate Two. He has talked about his heavy drinking and how he downs a fifth like most people drink a beer. He says it take two or three fifths to make him drunk.

After chess, Cellmate One decided to clean the cell. There really wasn't anything to clean but Cellmate One was on it, meticulously doing every little thing. He took two hours to mop the floor with a rag. Then, he cleaned the rag and washed all the walls. Cellmate Two and I offered to help but Cellmate One had a specific way he wanted it done. He let Cellmate Two help but he just ignored my offer.

Cellmate Two saw what was going on and told me not to help. It was obvious that he saw how Cellmate One was treating me and decided not to push the issue. Besides, it gave them something to do during lockdown. The situation reminded me of a triad relationship that happens with little girls. Girls one and two are friends and when girl number three comes along;

girl number one picks her and ignores number two. I'm OK with the situation. It was interesting to observe and watch the dynamics. I suspect they will evolve into something different but that's what they were today.

It reminded me of how our society views loyalty. We don't think we can have a relationship with a second person because of an existing relationship with a first person. Therefore, romantic relationships occur through serial monogamy. It goes back to the perspective of scarcity. The belief is that there is only one person for me or only one person at a time for me. What would happen if, instead of "owning" one person, we had an abundance perspective and loved many?

Today, I'm reading Margaret Craven's *I Heard the Owl Call My Name*. The novel moves slowly. In spite of this, it is enchanting. It tells the story of a young vicar assigned to Indians in the northwestern United States. It reminds me of spending time in here. Things move painfully slowly and there doesn't appear to be an end in sight.

At the end of chapter eleven, there is a quote that deeply touches my heart. It brings great insight into my current situation. It brings significant hope and encouragement to me. It explains how this situation will bring us new friends and solidify relationships within our family. "You suffered with them, and now you are theirs, and nothing will ever be the same again."

This quote tells me that the slowness of this situation is the suffering. I can only communicate by fifteen-minute phone calls, twenty-minute video visits, and handwritten letters. The instant world of internet and cell phones is not available to me, so my help to my friends and family is limited. They are suffering with me. I'm sure the result of this will be a significant change when I will become theirs. They will own me, not in the "control me" sense of the word, but in the support one another definition of the word. In our hearts and minds, we will see the connection and we will support one another because we will be in each other's hearts and minds. The slowness of today will evolve into a quantum leap of efficiency in accomplishing the dreams and goals of peace and beingness.

I understand that we must "be" first before we can do and have. I'm confident in my being and I Desire likeminded people to join me. This situation creates a void so they can do so. Some people are leaving, some are staying, new people are joining. Others will join or rejoin us in the future, including the children who cannot communicate with us today. I don't know how this will happen and I don't have to know the how. All I know is that the vision given to me in 1984 will come to pass. All I have to do is be who I am.

Our openness in sharing this suffering with others, including our children, contrasts sharply with how my parents and The Wife's parents did not allow us to experience their suffering. They hid their suffering from us and did not give us the opportunity to connect with them on a deep level. Of course, we saw their suffering even when they wouldn't share it or allow us to invest in them. Their efforts to protect us put a barrier between us and them. Maybe they thought we would judge them. Maybe they thought we didn't need to help them. Maybe they were ashamed of their situations. Whatever the case, they hid their suffering from us and didn't allow us to share it; therefore, we couldn't share in their lives at a deep level.

It is another example of openness versus hiding and the associated results. Hiding prevents progress. Openness allows progress to flourish.

I'm thinking of this as I write detailed instructions to my kids about how to handle my finances. I don't know how long I will be in here. However, I still have significant financial obligations leftover from two failed businesses. I will do everything I can to meet those obligations, including giving my children the instructions they need to help me with this. I can't imagine my parent's or The Wife's parents doing this. I suppose they would if they had to do so but it would feel strange because they wouldn't honestly talk with us about money. It is natural to talk to our children about money because we have talked about it each week. They know what we make, who we owe, the amounts of our bills. They know it all and they have access to all of it.

Of course, our parents may have known that suffering sorts some people out of our lives and glues others into our lives. They may have not been comfortable with the thought of this, so they hid the suffering so the sorting and gluing couldn't take place. As for me, I know that change is how the world functions and that it is futile to fight it. Instead, I must embrace change and watch the results. Truthfully, I look forward to seeing the results of this change. I look forward to seeing who will stay and who will go.

That doesn't mean it isn't emotional. As the day in lockdown continued, my emotions hung on edge. Someone would say "cookies" and I'd think of Daughter Two's homemade cookies. I'd hear something on TV about New Year's Day and I'd think about our anniversary. The slightest thing would associate with my life outside of here and I would experience the rush of emotions associated with wanting to be out of this damn place.

I take some comfort in the fact that the holidays will end and business will be back to normal in thirty-six hours. Hopefully, the courts will move quickly and people can move out of here. Specifically, I hope my attorney can work a miracle and get us out of here.

I finished my twenty-four hours in this cell by reading a romance novel. I thought it was a business book when I got it but it wasn't. There are no mistakes so the message spoke to me about love over business. It's a good message. It also spoke to me about love versus convenience – another good message!

Sunday, January 2, 2011

Lockdown continued today. At least we can have visits during lockdown. Daughter One and My Helper came to visit me. My Helper has decided to run my business while I'm in here. We even talked about the possibility of continuing that relationship afterwards. We'll see how it evolves.

Several years ago, we had an old Ford van that was on its last legs. The transmission was about to go and, since I was coaching basketball at the time, I wasn't spending much time with my business. That meant I wasn't making much money, so repairing the van wasn't in the budget. We used the van to transport the team and there were many times when I was afraid the van might not finish the trip.

Every time I started to worry about it, God would ask, "Do you trust me?" I would think about that question as I drove. I would think about that question when the van struggled up one of New Mexico's hills. I would think about that question every time I heard a funny sound from under the hood.

I always answered that question "yes" and we always got home safely.

Even at the end of a holiday vacation, when the van lost the top gear in the transmission and our family was faced with a Christmas Eve drive from Phoenix to Albuquerque in 2nd gear, I heard that question. I remembered thinking about all those other times I trusted and once again, I answered "yes." It took us three hours longer than we had planned. However, we arrived home safely after the final trip in that van.

The past few days, when my emotions have reached an edge and I have wanted to run out of here, I have once again heard the voice of God saying, "Do you trust me?" It is the same voice, the same tone, the same confidence.

I hear that question and I think about the past. I think about my current situation. I think about everything facing me. In spite of these thoughts, I know nothing has changed. God is God. I am me. Our relationship is the same. I trust and I know all is well. I answer yes.

It reminds me that we often experience one thing to prepare us for the next. God is gentle. God doesn't put us in fearful situations. God moves us forward gently, without coercion, so we can experience what we need to experience to be all we can be in this lifetime.

Lockdown finally ended at 4 this afternoon. It was good to be out of the cell. The lockdown ended my streak of 180 days with The Five Tibetans. I performed this routine every day from June 1 through December 31. I found it interesting that it took not having a place large enough to do the routine to end my consecutive days of doing it. I have considered doing something else. However, I have found nothing else that soothes my body and provides the flexibility available through doing TFT.

I decided I'll continue the routine in here. I'll adjust it to this environment but I'll continue with it. I may add some things to it but that's the only adjustment I see. I want to spend more time working out in here but it's tough because the schedule in the POD is erratic. In PAC 2, I had time alone and could almost control my day. In here, there is a lot to do and little time alone.

Truthfully, there is no time alone. This helps the time go by faster but I can't spend as much time doing the self-help stuff I was doing in PAC 2.

I wrote quite a bit about evil the other day, especially in regards to Head Counselor's thoughts and Peck's writing. I realized today that what they call "evil" is really tied to love. I say this because of the realization that everything is an act of love or a cry for love. Therefore, when Cellmate One is ignoring me, it is a cry for love. When he obsesses about anything, it is a cry for love. When Fighter Pilot says "niggers," it is a cry for love. When guys brag about their next fight, high, or act of revenge, it is a cry for love. When large institutions such as those associated with correction, religion, or medicine attempt to control others, it is a cry for love.

When Religious Guy picks on guys at the card table, becomes self-righteous about his reading material, and criticizes his spades partner, it is a cry for love.

My after-dinner routine consists of playing spades with Fighter Pilot, Religious Guy and whoever my partner is. Fighter Pilot and Religious Guy are always partners. They recruited me to play with them because they needed an "intelligent adversary who wouldn't giggle." I don't care if I win or not and I'm not testy about how the game is played. I just play.

Religious Guy is an expert player (if you don't believe it, just ask him) and he often picks on my various partners about their mistakes and criticizes Fighter Pilot when he makes a rare error. I need to remember that his negative statements at the card table are a cry for love.

Monday, January 3, 2011

Depression comes without warning in jail. If it isn't recognized and dealt with quickly, it piles on like a load of bricks. Each brick feels heavier than the previous one and each one hits the pile quicker than the last one and each until a person is buried. At that point, it doesn't matter what happens next. The depression has set in and it will stay for a while, maybe longer. Kind words bring tears. Harsh words bring anger. The only way out for me is to process, think through it, back up, and gain perspective. That's why I write.

I awoke today to find my mind actively reviewing the events leading up to my arrest. I thought about how unfair it was and how this is a waste of time. I used meditation to connect with the Divine to submit to the Universe's purpose for me to be here. That helped but the depression lingered.

I called Daughter One and the connection was awful. She couldn't hear me most of the time and she broke down halfway through the call. It was then that I realized she was running this as a sprint, not a marathon. Of course, I couldn't tell her that because of the connection. I got a picture of how hard this is for her and for everyone in our family. I felt responsible for their struggle as the depression descended.

She told me she heard The Wife laugh during her phone call with her yesterday. That gave me a little lift in the depression but it didn't last long.

Today is the day for church service and The Preacher came and wished me "Happy Anniversary." He also told me my kids helped them move a bunch of stuff Saturday. He thanked me for their help. I wanted to ask him if he had ever spent time in jail, especially an anniversary and if he knew that pain. I wanted to ask him if he understood that when you're in jail, you cope by pushing aside the pain of the things you're missing and when someone brings it up, it's like ripping a scab off a wound.

Instead, I smiled, thanked him for his comments and his invitation to today's service, and continued playing cards as another brick went onto the pile. I knew he meant well, but that didn't help me at all.

After being in here almost four weeks, I've decided that anyone who works in here, volunteers, or otherwise interacts with inmates should spend a minimum of two weeks as a prisoner to see what it is like. The emotional and mental stress and the maturity required to handle that stress cannot be understood any other way.

When I went to take my shower today, a young man was on the other side. I noticed he kept looking at me to see if I was watching him. Once he was satisfied that I wasn't, he turned his back to me. As my shower progressed, I realized he was pleasuring himself. I ignored him, finished my shower, and quickly left.

Our CO for the past two days has been P. She is the one who was so afraid of me in PAC2. She's a bully, full of fear, and profanities. She previously worked as a stripper and even though she isn't comfortable in here, she loves bossing people around. I suspect she has a hidden desire to be a dominatrix.

One thing is for sure. Having her for a CO is not a good remedy for my depression.

When joy comes, it comes at unexpected moments. Depression makes me stoic. I become hard. I stare. I don't smile. Joy makes me giddy. When it really hits me, I cry.

Tonight, before dinner. I played Rummy with Fighter Pilot, Religious Guy, and another inmate. Mail came during that time and I received a letter from The Wife; the first direct communication with her since December 9 – almost four weeks. I was amazed at how much her letter lifted my spirits and improved my mood. Suddenly Fighter Pilot, Religious Guy, and I were trading stories and everyone was in a good mood. We even noticed that The Horned Owl was doing laps around the POD.

The Horned Owl is an older gentleman with long thin hair that hangs halfway down his back and very long fingernails. He has dark bushy eyebrows and the outer edge of each sticks up. That, combined with the long, thin hair, coming off a mostly bald head, makes him look like a sick, horned owl; one that can no longer fly because he is losing his feathers. He always waits until everyone is done to walk up to the medicine cart because he isn't able to stand in line while everyone else gets their meds. His steps are always slow; as if he isn't sure he will be able to take the next one. The first time I saw him, I wondered if he would survive his stay in here. Religious Guy told me he has seen The Horned Owl's physical condition deteriorate over the past several months.

I've eaten at the same table with him almost every day and never once has he acknowledged me or even looked up when I or anyone else joined him at the table. To see The

Horned Owl walk around the POD was certainly a change, I'd never seen him even have the energy to smile, much less walk.

At dinner, I again joined him and two other gentlemen at the table. I chatted with the guy on the left and when I looked up at The Horned Owl, he looked up at me. I nodded and he smiled slightly. That smile radiated out from his lips, shined from his eyes, and suddenly my vision went blurry.

All day, the emotions, the depression, the joy from The Wife's letter, and everything else culminated in that moment as I experienced love from the depth of his being. It was subtle and yet it was so bold. It was as if God, Goddess, and the Universe had unleashed all the love in the world on me. A jailhouse dinner never tasted better.

Tuesday, January 4, 2011

Today was normal, for a day in jail. A good phone call with Daughter One, writing letters, playing cards, a workout, and shower all combined to make the day go by quickly. We had a good conversation over cards about the legal system and how to improve it. We all walked away with something to think about.

I wrote The Wife today and invited her to reach me by astral travel. I had some success with that in PAC2. Having cell mates who are noisy at bed time made that difficult for me at first. However, I'm learning their patterns so I'm figuring out how to insert my spiritual practices in this POD. I received a letter of support today from The Revolutionary. He wants to change the judicial system and so do I. He says he is "devoting his life to finding and supporting people being railroaded by the system - once he gets out."

I went outside this morning to do part of my workout. As I started, a crow flew overhead and cawed good morning to me. While playing cards, I noticed the crow again. Then a second one appeared. They flew, hovered, played, dove, and even landed on the parking lot light pole I can see from SEG1. I could see so little sky and yet, they stayed in my vision for more than five minutes. I have to believe they were celebrating the fact that The Wife and I are writing each other.

Wednesday, January 5, 2011

I continued to find my rhythm today. I showered, got in a full workout plus some extra stuff, and started work on Peace of Mind Training Institute Workshops. I am pleased that I've decided on another project to do while I'm in here. The Peace of Mind Training Institute project will take me quite a while to complete so I feel peaceful about being here and having the time to do that work. In addition, it helps me stay focused on why I'm here – at least the larger, UNIVERSAL reason I'm here. It is a boost to my spiritual perspective and makes me excited to be here!

Thursday, January 6, 2011

    I learned about fear yesterday during my Peace of Mind Training Institute writing.

    Fear is a powerful emotion. We often think of it as something we would rather avoid because it is the opposite of love. We tend to run from things we are afraid of. However, that fear and the related emotion and energy that come from running from it actually work to do two things. First, the "real fear" (that which we know in our being is part of our life plan) prepares us to experience events that we are afraid of so that when we experience them, we aren't afraid of them. Second, it actually attracts those things to us.

    For example, after our first arrest, we were afraid of jail time and of losing our children. The whole process of police knocking at the door at 1 AM and entering without permission or warrant, CYFD investigation, arrest, jail time, paying bond, hiring an attorney, and dealing with the related emotions hung with me all the time. My pulse increased every time I saw a squad car and I replayed possible scenarios between me and law enforcement officers.

    My fear seemed irrational to me so I didn't think it was "real fear." I used everything I knew to use to quell the fear and I couldn't make it go away permanently because every time I encountered the next police officer or squad car, the fear returned. Losing my family, our house, or our businesses didn't bring fear to me. Being robbed or mugged or killed didn't bring fear to me. The only thing I was afraid of was law enforcement

That's why I call it "real fear." I couldn't dump it. God doesn't desire for us to experience fear. Therefore, when we cannot overcome a fear, we must experience something to relieve it. The system that causes this to work has at least two parts.

The first part is the plan I make with God before coming to this life. That plan is for me to become love. To become love, I must work through my fears. My personal fears have to do with love, romance, and intimacy. As I've worked through those fears, I've discovered others related to loss of freedom. Maybe I died in jail in a previous life. Maybe I couldn't love the people I wanted to love in another life. Therefore, I picked this life to overcome those fears.

The second part is the Law of Attraction at work. As I experience the emotion of fear, I actually attract the things I'm afraid of through the principle of sympathetic vibration. This isn't a punishment because I've committed the sin of fear. It is how I release fear so I can become love. In my current situation, I know that when I leave jail, I will be freer to love because I've faced this fear.

This idea about fear is consistent with what the Bible teaches in the Book of Job. Job adds some Hebrew sacrifices into the equation and he has some miserable comforters who try to convince him of his sin. However, he didn't sin. He only had a "real fear" that he had to experience. His miserable comforters tried to equate the results in Job's life to some sin he had committed when, in truth, there was something else happening. Job was being delivered of fear while his comforters were being delivered of equating financial and circumstantial results with spirituality.

Job's comforters remind me of those people who judged our current situation and said, "It happened because you don't go to church." Like Job's friends, they have a limited worldview. Our response, like Job's response, is to hold to what we know to be truth. We can love them and be gracious to them without giving up our truth.

That's what I did yesterday when Preacher Two, from Light and Liberty, visited. (Fighter Pilot calls him "Bible Thumper.") He had talked to The Mother-in-Law and she wanted him to come see me. I was gracious, friendly, and unbending in my unwillingness to attend his meeting. I guess I see myself as Job and the prison ministers as my "miserable comforters" who want to tie my incarceration to sin rather than recognizing it as God's way of helping me become love by overcoming fear.

Cellmate One has begun to acknowledge me. I think he was unsure about me at first, afraid maybe, and now that he has gotten to know me and my behaviors, he is relaxed around me. I enjoy the entertainment of his obsessive and compulsive behavior. When I arrived in this POD, he explained to me that because of the loud noise associated with the flushing of the toilets, we should say "fire in the hole" prior to flushing. Over the past week, the term has changed to "fire" to "flushing" to "shitter." I just smile.

He told me today that several people in the POD have been his cellmates. He said they moved out for various reasons but he wouldn't tell me what they were except to say that they couldn't handle his obsessive behavior.

"I know I'm obsessive but it is just who I am and I don't hurt anyone with it."

I didn't tell him what others had said about him. Several of his former cellmates have approached me and asked what it is like to live with Cellmate One.

"So far, so good."

"I couldn't stand living with him because he was so mean."

"Oh?"

"Yes, if you don't follow his rules about cleaning the cell, he goes off on you. He's an asshole. He just makes your life miserable. I couldn't stand it. "

Friday, January 7, 2011

The Beard sometimes joins us at our card table. He is a few years older than me. He told us yesterday that he is a former Marine. I wouldn't have guessed it because he doesn't fit the macho image of a marine. He is sarcastic, wears a long beard that he often transforms into a long pony tail that hangs from his chin.

Today, he told us a story about his basic training. He said their physical training instructor was a jerk and his unit decided they would exhaust him one day. They decided to do this by running all day with the instructor. They ran from six in the morning until nine or ten at night. He said they ran in formation and the other units sprayed them with a water hose for drinks. They must have run 100 miles and he said it was awful but it worked. The PT instructor wasn't such a jerk in the future. I didn't understand how the unit could control the instructor that way but it was a funny story.

He received a letter this week from his sister. He told us there are a lot of women in his life. Eight sisters and three ex-wives and they all get along.

"It sounds like estrogen overload to me."

"I have a brother."

"That helps balance it out."

"Not really. He's gay."

I suppose there are some gay inmates in here but I only see one that's obvious. We call him Girl Guy. He wears his hair like a girl and acts like a girl. He doesn't bother anyone or at least he hasn't so far.

Fighter Pilot calls one group of guys "the queers" because they like to "touch." They're always shaking hands with people and patting them on the back. The touching is normal for our society. It doesn't mean the guys are gay. It means they are human beings participating in acts of love by being friendly.

Fighter Pilot, by his own admission is "a stoic." He has chosen to repress his desire for touch and love so that he will not be disappointed when those desires are not met. I suspect that is why he is so quick to lash out and label others. Repressing desires doesn't make the desires go away. Instead, those desires build up inside of a person until they explode in a violent manner.

The violence can sometimes be drastic and manifest as murder or other physical harm. However, in most cases, the violence is subtle. It may be a verbal eruption. It may be expressed through physical labor. It may be demonstrated through being aloof. Whatever the method of expression, it is a cry for love.

Over the past couple of days, I've thought a lot about why I am afraid to love. There are many reasons ranging from fear of rejection to judgment of others to our society's preference for violence over love. As a society, we actually discourage people from being loving. We tell a man his lover is too old, too young, to rich, too poor, too skinny, or too fat for him. We tell a woman her lover is the wrong color, wrong sex, or wrong race for her.

I've noticed that, in most cases, once a man enters into a relationship, he tries to control that person. He attempts to force that person into his mold. He hides part of himself away so the other person can't get to know him. This behavior isn't limited to men. A woman does the same thing and the resulting conflicts rage.

Our society is so dysfunctional when it comes to love that we no longer understand healthy love. Therefore, we have created significant marriage, divorce, and custody laws to regulate it. These laws are so nvolved and complex that they become more important and we spend more time trying to use those laws to get our way than we do actually loving. Is it any wonder that we fear love so much?

I talked to Daughter One today and she's getting a tattoo on her shoulder today. It is a dragonfly and some shooting stars. I'm stoked about it and I look forward to seeing it. Daughter One is mature and flighty at the same time. I love that about her. She does things many people consider impulsive and she has learned to do that in a responsible manner.

She told me a couple of other things today too that brought me tears of joy. She said food continues to show up on the front door step, usually without notes. She also told me about a visit she and Motorcycle Rider's Wife had with The Wife.

Motorcycle Rider and Motorcycle Rider's Wife have eight kids and gave up on traditional church several years ago. We hung out together for a couple of years, however, as our belief system changed, we didn't get together as much; primarily because I saw them as extremely conservative. After chatting with Daughter One today, I see that I misjudged them.

(Isn't it interesting that all judgments are misjudgments?) Motorcycle Rider's Wife told Daughter One that they had a situation similar to ours with one of their kids and if someone had gone to the authorities, they would be in jail. She said she'd want support if she was in here so she came to visit The Wife. When the visit was over, she went to the canteen and put $40 on each of our accounts.

I'm not sure when or if I'll need that because College Friend placed another internet order for me. I have enough snacks, phone cards, and envelopes for several weeks. There is abundance, even in jail! ☺

At least one other person sees the abundance here. It is The Dumpster Diver. I'm not sure why he isn't in a Psych POD because he certainly qualifies. His diagnosis is schizophrenia and his favorite pastime is collecting brightly colored snack wrappers from the trash can. I watched him approach a full trash bag today after a BO had tied it closed and placed it by the sally port door. I thought for a moment that The Dumpster Diver was going to open it and go through it. Instead, he mumbled something, probably cursing his missed opportunities, and walked away in disgust.

One of the favorite words in here, especially for the younger inmates, is "Dawg." They use that term when they want to be "chummy" with someone. Such as, "Hey Dawg, can I have a shot of coffee" or "Hey Dawg, you want a soup?" The pronunciation sounds like Georgia, which is funny because the Hispanics use the term the most and their accent sounds nothing like a Deep South accent.

Today, during my shower, I heard someone yell, "Hey CO, fight!" I braced for the worst but I guess it was minor. I don't know if the POD will earn lockdown because of it or not. Cellmate One thinks so. I don't. Today's CO was cool, no crazy stuff like some of the other guys. One CO, R, goes through a couple times a day and locks all the doors. He doesn't care if we are in or out of the cells; he just wants the doors locked. I can't figure out why he does it and the other inmates say he does it just to mess with us.

While waiting to use the phone today, one inmate started talking to me about his "cancer." He is sure he is dying of it. As he talked, I noticed his yellowish skin color and eye whites and surmised that he could have cancer although I have no way to confirm that. I had to ask myself what happens if you get cancer while you're in jail. I know MDC has a medical department so I guess he could be treated there. However, I can't imagine them doing chemotherapy or anything similar.

Speaking of health issues, the fire alarm continues to go off at random times throughout the day and night. Fighter Pilot, Religious Guy, and I discussed the merits of a class action lawsuit over that issue. I don't suppose a lawsuit would be worth the effort but it was a fun discussion.

Saturday, January 8, 2011

"Put up your hands, this is a hold up." There was a finger in my back and the voice pretended to be serious.

"What do you want?" I responded between bites of food.

"Your cookies."

I smiled as Shiny Eye sat down beside me while I finished lunch. Shiny Eye lives in the cell next door and he's always smiling. He has a dark eye and an eye with a vertical streak of white down the middle of the iris. It could be a marble eye for all I know. It makes him look like an angel with light radiating from his eyes.

Even though I was in jail, with more than ninety accused criminals, the "hold up" didn't increase my pulse or cause me worry. I was not afraid. I had overcome that fear.

After our 9 AM lunch, we were locked down for the rest of the day so I had a chance to think and write. It appeared that weekend lockdown was the usual practice in this POD. At least we were out of our cells during the week.

I've thought about fear a lot over the past few days. I've considered whether fear, "real fear," is a part of God. I've considered whether a fear workshop would cause more fear because "what we focus on expands." I've considered that God uses the technique of encouraging us to lean into the fear to overcome it. When all was considered, I decided a fear workshop would be a good idea so I started putting it together. It is good to face fears.

Cellmate One is doing that and we're starting to get along. I realized yesterday that he was ignoring me because he was afraid of me. I suppose my self-confidence and calm demeanor can be intimidating at times. About a week ago, Cellmate One and I had a conversation about the vent in our room. The air circulation system at MDC has a fan that runs all the time. The outflow vent is in the wall, under the desk. It blows air towards the door and into the commons area. The bunk beds are on the wall opposite the airflow so the air doesn't directly hit the bed area. However, when a third, portable bunk is put into the cell, it goes on the floor and the air blows directly onto that bed. My bunk is in that position on the floor and the air can be cool at times and downright cold at other times.

Our conversation was about redirecting or blocking the vent so the air wouldn't blow directly on me. When I mentioned it to Cellmate One, he overreacted and told me to use my blankets or move out of the room. I apologized and told him I didn't mean any harm. It was just a suggestion.

Since then, I've started bundling up to stay warm, sleeping with my sheet over my head and using my pillow blanket to wrap up when I wasn't sleeping. I didn't say another word about the vent.

Yesterday, after I received my order from commissary, I realized I had more stuff than I needed. I heard Cellmate One say he needed a wash cloth, so I gave him one. I also gave him a pair of boxer shorts and we shared some popcorn last night. When I went to bed last night, I bundled up as always and was suddenly too warm. I uncovered and noticed that Cellmate One had covered the vent with the trashcan.

One of the most stereotypical guys in here is The Leprechaun. He is short, has the little green guy's facial hair below his round cheeks, and giggles a lot. He loves Notre Dame and the Boston Celtics. He also has the Notre Dame mascot tattooed on his bicep. I think he really believes he is a Leprechaun.

Sunday, January 9, 2011

We remained under lockdown longer than usual this morning. The reason had something to do with Girl Guy. After quite a bit of activity around his cell, a Sergeant came in and escorted him out of the POD while the CO grabbed his property box. Girl Guy had something around his neck when he left but I couldn't tell if he was injured.

What I found out later is that Girl Guy has converted the sleeve from one of his thermal shirts into a scarf to keep his neck warm. The CO wanted him to take off the scarf. Girl Guy wouldn't do that so the CO called the Sergeant, had Girl Guy transferred to a real segregation POD, and locked down our POD.

From my perspective, t was a random, barbaric act done by a female CO. I've noticed the female COs feel like they have something to prove, so they are always doing crazy things to mess with the inmates, like locking down the entire POD because one inmate, who has been removed, was disrespectful.

The entire concept of lockdown reeks of control and power. The goal of this facility isn't to help the inmates. It is to warehouse us and keep us off-balance by mixing up things so that we understand we're not in control. They cage us like animals, feed us through the door, and leave the fire alarm in a state of disrepair to torture us with noise at all times of the day and night.

The COs and other staff are afraid of us. They're outnumbered here 90 to 1. They either ignore us or over-control us. There is no interaction and little trust. What if, instead of their current system, they gave us consistent interaction; let us use our energies in a positive, life-giving manner, so that those who had abilities could use them for something other than playing games, watching TV, and reading books?

Our efforts could be rewarded with quicker resolutions of the cases for people who cooperate so that people who want to stay in here could stay and others could earn their way out. It wouldn't be measured by time. It would be measured by results.

I chatted with Fighter Pilot tonight about his future. I knew he was headed to prison and I hoped it was for a short time. What I discovered is that he is serving his prison sentence here because the courts have lost his papers. He is glad to be here instead of there because it is more convenient for his wife of 52 years.

"How much time do you have left?"

"Quite a bit."

"Oh... I had hoped to see you on the outside at some point in the future."

"That isn't likely."

My vision blurred. "That's pretty crappy."

I'd heard him use that term twice. Once when he heard about my charges and once when he heard about The Wife's living arrangements in MDC. He understood my use of the term.

"Yeah, pretty crappy."

Monday, January 10, 2011

"Cox, you have court today. You wanna get a shower?"

"Yes, please."

Of course, I wanted to get a shower. After yesterday's lockdown, I didn't bother to shower because I didn't want to wait in line. Ninety men, using four shower stalls, at fifteen minutes per shower would take five hours to shower. We were out of our cells for four hours. Subtract an hour for dinner and medications and I decided I cou d miss one day's shower.

I got up, grabbed the disposable razor the CO had left on the chuck door, and started shaving. Shaving was interrupted by breakfast. After breaking, I finished shaving during my shower.

While showering, I noticed a red place on my left hip. It was scabbed over. I didn't remember hitting anything. Then I realized it was a bedsore. I alternate sleeping on my back and on my side. I had noticed some pain on my left hip but I didn't consider the possibility of a bedsore. I was almost angry. They warehouse us on mattresses so thin that we can't sleep on them without pain. It was inhumane.

I allowed the water to wash away my emotions while I took a deep breath and relaxed, knowing I could sleep on my back and let the sore heal.

I came back to the cell, and dressed as everyone had recommended.

"Wear a T-shirt because the van to court is cold. Wear two pairs of socks to protect your ankles from the shackles."

Now, I wait for transportation to court, wondering what today will bring. I had hoped Substitute Attorney would visit me prior to today and educate me on this process but she didn't. I assume she will be there today and we'll chat, but I don't know that. I've been told that court was in Metro Court the first two times and now, it is in District Court. I've been told to avoid certain judges. I've been told that my bond could go up and it could go down. If it goes down enough, we might be able to get out of here. I wonder if that's even possible. I wonder if Substitute Attorney worked her contacts to arrange for our release or if all of that will happen today.

Today is another chapter of this adventure. I'll wait and see what happens, knowing without doubt, that it is a "Conspiracy For Me."

Monday, January 10, 2011 (PM)

What happened today was a bunch of nothing. I went to transport, rode the van to court, and watched other people's arraignments. The judge seemed fair while ruling on the other cases. I sat there and watched for a couple of hours because Substitute Attorney didn't show up. The judge had no choice but to continue the hearing until next week. The TV cameras were there. The cameramen only shot film of The Wife and me. Otherwise, they did nothing.

I saw The Wife; talked to her briefly, bumped her a time or two, winked, blew kisses, and encouraged her to relax. She was upset that Substitute Attorney didn't show up. I understood but there was nothing we could do so I didn't worry about it. I assumed it was all part of the "Conspiracy for Me."

As I walked out the door to the van this morning, I looked up and saw crows, dozens of them. They were there to encourage me, let me know they were watching over me, and working on my behalf. I knew immediately that they represented the army of beings both physical and non-physical, who were working on our behalf. I just didn't know how they were working. I found out when I called Daughter One.

She told me Substitute Attorney was both angry and ecstatic about some events that happened this morning. First of all, no one notified her of the court time, so she didn't know to show up. She was angry about that. Secondly, the detective called and threatened to arrest our older children because they sent Christmas presents to the younger ones. Prior to our arrest, we had already received permission to give them presents so Substitute Attorney thinks this is harassment and she may consider an action against him. Third, Substitute Attorney is working with a bail bondsman on the possibly of a property bond to get us out and said we could be out as soon as Tuesday of next week. I'm not counting on it, but it is interesting.

Mail call had four letters today including two from Substitute Attorney. She filed motions regarding my bond and getting the computers from the Sheriff's office. I'm pleased.

I talked to Shiny Eye last night about his eye. He said when he was in 8th grade, he was in shop, and one guy threw a metal triangle to another guy. Of course, triangles have a tendency to curve and the errant throw hit him in the eye. It damaged his eye and he lost his vision. I told him it looked like a bright light coming from his eye and I saw him as an angel. He was blown away. I don't think anyone had called him an angel before.

The emotions of the day have left me drained. I'm working on not attaching to the results and just being.

216

Tuesday, January 11, 2011

When meditation is done correctly, I'm able to step outside myself and observe. One of my observations this morning is that I'm now afraid of leaving this environment. Not afraid as in I won't leave when the opportunity presents itself, but afraid as in what I will do when I leave.

For example, My Helper moved into our master bedroom yesterday. She starts running my business today, so she will move into my office today. How will I pay her once I get out? What is fair to her, fair to us? When will we get the computers? Which clients will I try to recover? Will they all leave? Will any leave? Will any stay?

If I get out on bond, how long will I be out of custody? Will I be convicted and when will that take place? Will I be acquitted? Will I be given the opportunity to make a reasonable plea? Will I be on probation? There are so many questions and, of course, none of them have answers today because they don't need to have answers today.

As I write these words, some ideas come to me. I need to have My Helper and Daughter One do the monthly work while I do the extra stuff, go get clients, and write books. They benefit from my expertise while I expand other parts of the business. In addition, if I go back into custody at some point, the primary business can continue without me. Obviously, if they are working, there will be money to pay them because we'll be making income. And, based on how people are supporting us even in here, I can assume people will support us once we are released.

I suppose this would be a good time to say that when journaling is done correctly, it allows me to resolve things observed during meditation.

Of course, there are other things to consider besides my business and my changes. I think the thing that shakes me most is relationships. Who will stay? What role will each person play? Which family members will come back? Which will go? I suppose that's always been the way it is so this shouldn't be any different. The truth is that those who currently have a relationship with me will always have a relationship with me. Relationships don't end. They change form over time. The form changes as each individual chooses to spend less time or more time with me. My arrest and incarceration is just another element to consider if someone is going to have a relationship with me.

I also noticed that my "warrior spirit" is strong today. I still struggle with that term. The only alternative I've come up with is "negotiator" although that doesn't seem to pack the same punch as "warrior." "Ambassador" is OK but it sounds too political. One word I've always liked is "emissary." Maybe I should use that.

It reminds me of James Twyman's writings and The Emissaries of Light that use their meditation in warring areas to create peace. It reminds me of the powerful stories told in his books *Emissary of Light* and *Emissary of Love.* For me, the word "emissary" is powerful, mystical, and miraculous. YES. That's it - I'll call my "warrior spirit" my "emissary spirit"

My emissary spirit is ready to bring peace to me, my family, and others who desire to associate with me. If someone attempts to disrupt that peace, we will take the steps necessary to resolve that, while recognizing the cry for love.

I noticed that being in jail has similarities to being in the military. There are uniforms, set schedules (often changed), someone in absolute control, shared experiences that produce camaraderie, bland food, time to serve, and the uncertainty of what's next. I suppose that only stands to reason since any government entity that's designed to control through intimidation must have certain systems in place. This isn't to say that the systems are bad. It is to say that when attempting to control other people, there must be absolutes, especially absolute control.

The problem with this is that God is so creative and the Universe is so varied in its processes that absolutes don't work. Therefore, each person in a given situation must be ready, willing, and able to communicate, to offer input on what might work. This input must have behind it an attitude that doesn't care who gets credit for the results as long as the process produces the desired results.

Large systems, like corrections, military, and even religions do it "that way" because they've always done it that way. They're big, cumbersome, and difficult to change. Therefore, results are often forgotten and the input of all is often neglected. This produces a society where there has to be a boss who is always "right." This leads to abuse as those in power forget to consider those under their power.

Cellmate One is a modest example of that. He has often referred to his "life on the streets." That's a term we all use in here to refer to life outside of jail. To him, it really is life on the streets. He is homeless. None of his family has living arrangements where he can participate so he lives in homeless shelters or in a motel when he can earn money from "side jobs." He likes to dress well and eat well so he spends his money on clothing and food. He likes to drink so he purchases booze too.

I realize his cell situation with Cellmate Two and me is as close as he's been to living with someone in quite a while. His obsessive and compulsive cleaning had actually run off his previous cell mates and he had a cell by himself before Cellmate Two arrived. No one gets a cell to themselves in this POD but he managed to do so. I tried to imagine his life on the streets and realized life in jail is safer for him because there are absolutes that he has to follow. In here, his choices are limited so it is more difficult for him to make "bad ones." I tried to imagine a way to help him on the streets and I couldn't find one. I could only feel compassion for him.

When we play spades after dinner, I find that my mind locks in and I play really well. It is as if my mind needs something puzzling to work on each day. Playing cards is it. Reading and writing during the day gives me opportunity to experience expression. However, it doesn't use the "math side" of my brain. I find it interesting to see how my mind works and adapts to this situation. Games certainly fill my minds need to solve puzzles. It's a nice diversion, although I must admit I'd rather puzzle over business ideas.

The Horned Owl continues to improve. He now walks laps every day, speaks to me during meals, and he is eating better. I noticed he even trimmed his nails and took a shower. I still remember that spark of love that radiated out of his eyes last week. I wonder where that came from. I wonder how he transformed himself at that moment.

Taking care of my body is a little bit of a challenge in here because everything is hard. The seats are steel, the doors are steel, the sinks, toilets, and desks are steel. Everything is steel except for my bunk. It's hard plastic. If I accidently bump something, even if I do it gently, it hurts...a lot. I've done that to my right leg three times producing three lumps: One the size of a marble and two the size of Ping-Pong balls.

Through the discomfort, I've managed to keep my back healthy through doing TFT. The flexibility required for this routine allows me to easily self-adjust my back and relieve any pain.

Another challenge is the digestion of jail food. The keys to digestion success are lots of water and exercise. Again, this isn't so different from life on the outside. Once again, I credit TFT for the way it massages my abdomen and aids digestion.

The hardness of jail speaks to me at so many levels. I have to remain aware or I notice it begins to harden me as it speaks. The discomfort speaks to my butt as I sit on the metal seats at the table while eating and playing cards. It speaks to my back as I lean against the concrete wall while I write. It speaks to my ears as the cold air rushes out of the cell's vent. It speaks to my arms as they go numb when I don't sleep in exactly the right position. It tells me that this place is designed for people to leave.

I've organized my stuff in here so that I can leave on a moment's notice and leave some stuff behind for Cellmate Two and Cellmate One. I'm ready to go. I've processed what I need to process from this perspective. I can work on Peace of Mind Training Institute workshops whether I'm in or out so I don't have to be in here to do them.

Wednesday, January 12, 2011

I awoke this morning with freedom energy pumping through my body. I did TFT and additional calisthenics, called Daughter One, talked with My Helper, and realized that things are under control. They aren't exactly as I want them but they are as God wants them so I must be content with that.

Then, the interruptions started. Command call for Captain. He's pleased with us. Command call for meds – a complete waste of time except for meditation. CO is back on his "keep the doors closed" kick so I can't get a shower yet.

When Freedom is pumping through me as it is today, I run on two emotional levels. One that says, "I'm free wherever I am at" and another that says, "I want to be out of here NOW!" This creates quite a conflict for me. Maybe not a conflict as much as a moodiness. I find my mood is best when I resolve to being here a long time and I never anticipate leaving. That keeps me in the moment and allows me to experience peace.

I'm reading *The Gift of Asher Lev*. It is about a Jewish artist who is famous, wealthy, and suddenly in a place where his life is out of his control. There are many similarities between us. He is separated from his family and facing events that take him to the next chapter of his life. The Rebbe, the leader of his religion, tells him "the more a thing is hidden from a man, the more he desires it."

The CO opened the doors, I showered, and I'm now in my cell writing because the doors are locked again. At least this gives us brief periods of privacy.

I wonder if something is hidden from me, something I can only find through this experience that I Desire so greatly that I created this situation to find it. Actually, I'm sure of this. I'm writing this journal. I'm creating the POMTI material. I'm growing softly strong in cracked places.

Cracked places that grow strong may not necessarily fill in the cracks. It is true they can fill in with scar tissue. Flesh wounds do this and so do trees. The scar tissue makes the crack stronger than the surrounding tissue. When The Wife repairs the interior of a car, the same thing happens. The repaired crack is usually stronger than the surrounding area.

However, in some cases, especially in art work such as sculptures, the cracks must remain and they must be strong because a crack is how the light gets in and out. If we consider the cracks in our soul, it is possible that enlightenment cannot happen without them. If they are strong, they won't break down when the elements go through them. If they are fragile, the cracks will become holes and possibly weaken to the point of destruction.

I feel a distance from The Wife today. It is as if she's faltering in our vision, our purpose. I wonder if it is a sign to me of something – not something disastrous but something none-the-less. I won't worry about it for now. I'll just observe it and see what happens.

Thursday, January 13, 2011

I have seen what it is doing and I'm beginning to understand. As I've read *The Gift of Asher Lev*, at a subconscious level, I became Asher, a gifted man, imprisoned by his gifts, rejected because of his gifts, and separated from his family because of his gifts. His Jewish Community rejects him just as many of those in my earlier Christian and fundamentalist community reject me.

Yet, each of us continues to work. His wife, Devorah, supports him but doesn't understand them and, even though she is fiercely loyal to him, she sides with the community regarding his work because she doesn't understand it. I see The Wife in Devorah. She is fiercely loyal to me. She is even fiercely loyal toward my work. She claims she understands it but maybe she doesn't, not on her own. It seems I have to be there to remind her how to apply it.

I see this as I read the book and I realize I am Asher. The Wife is Devorah. The similarities continue. Asher and Dev's youngest child, a boy, is Avrumel. He becomes the centerpiece of the book when the Rebbe decides Avrumel is to be Rebbe after Asher's father. (I really am not familiar with the term Rebbe. However, from the book, it appears that the Rebbe is to the Landover Hasidic community as the Pope is to the Catholics). I see Asher's Dad as The Wife's Dad and my youngest three kids are Avrumel.

As the book evolves, there is a conflict over where Avrumel will live and go to school. Will he stay in Brooklyn with his grandparents and the Rebbe? Or will he go back to France with his dad? There is a battle over the apparent spiritual callings of the young man and the parental longings of the dad. In the end, everyone stays in Brooklyn, except Asher. He must be true to his calling and he must work anywhere but Brooklyn.

Brooklyn is where the Jewish Community rejected him because of his controversial paintings, paintings that did not honor his Jewish Community. Of course, whenever a moral judgment is made, perspective is involved. This perspective, filtered by the judger's experience, decides good or evil, right or wrong. Unfortunately, this judgment seldom considers truth. In Asher's case, it was judged wrong, it was judged evil for him to use crucifixion to show the truth of suffering. In my case, it was judged wrong, it was judged evil for me to use nudity to show the truth of communication.

In addition, I'm certain The Wife's Dad, The Father-in-Law, sees this as a battle between good and evil, right and wrong, eternal life and eternal death, heaven and hell. He thinks he messed up with his five kids, the three girls he had with The Mother-in-Law and the two boys he adopted. The Wife married me. One of her sisters married a man who hides behind a mysterious disease. The other married a consistent follower who would rather play than work. However, he works at a state job he hates because retirement is just a few more years away. One of the adopted sons left home and died while incarcerated. The other managed to put together an unsettled life in Southeastern New Mexico.

I suspect The Father-in-Law doesn't see any success in his parenting skills. Now that he has three of our kids to work with, I'm sure he is attempting to make up for his previous perceived failures, if only at a subconscious level. I say subconscious level because I'm sure his conscious focus is on a war with the devil for the souls of our kids because he thinks the path I'm on is a "path to hell" and he doesn't want his grandchildren going down it.

For me, if I am Asher, must I separate from my family to do my work? Obviously, at least for the short term, the answer is "yes." I had hoped my kids would support me as I shared the Peace of Mind message. Now I realize the message must go forward with or without them. If they support me, I'm OK with that. If they don't, I'm OK with that.

My vision includes fifty people in three generations. I thought these would be biological people. I realized a few years ago, those people might not be biological. Many spiritual teachers talk about "the death of a vision" or "the law of opposites." These teachings always point to a time of suffering and loss that prepares us to accomplish the vision. I am certain this is one of those times.

I received my 2nd hair cut in jail today. I've now been here more than 5 weeks and it will be sometime next week at the earliest before I'm released. Court will be at 8:30 next Tuesday. Daughter One tells me she and Son Two will be there as part of the process to figure out a way to get us out of here.

I've noticed that the inmates do a remarkable job of handling the food trays. In more than five weeks of eating three meals a day, no one had dropped a tray until this week. This doesn't count the inmates in PAC 2 who purposely threw their trays across their cell or kicked them across the POD.

Food is really the only commodity we have to do business with in here. At first, I thought everyone would protect their stuff like crazy. Now, I see that it is like life on the outside. People have stuff and they want to bless other people with it. Fighter Pilot trades food for companionship. It is what older people do on the outside. They are lonely and they have stuff, have food, so they give food to someone for a few minutes of companionship. My cellmates and I give food to each other. One inmate gave a cup of coffee to the barber today while he was cutting my hair.

Spades became a little "testy" tonight. Religious Guy has a habit of bidding nil and expecting Fighter Pilot to cover him. When Fighter Pilot doesn't cover, Religious Guy makes a comment. Religious Guy is the type of guy who acts like he knows everything about everything so he often talks about his strategy and argues about who played what when it isn't in his best interest to do so. Tonight, when Fighter Pilot didn't cover him during a hand when he bid nil, he made a comment. Fighter Pilot threw down his hand; cards face up, and said, "Pick one!" It was obvious Fighter Pilot had only played what he had.

A little later, Religious Guy argued about what card I played. I played a lower card and we lost the trick. He insisted that someone else had played it and gave the trick to us. At the end of the hand, that trick cost his team the hand and subsequently they lost the game. It reminded me of something I heard a few years ago. "You can be rich or you can be right."

During our card games, Religious Guy has participated in numerous conversations about business, religion, and politics. He is so concerned with being "right" that he doesn't consider that the rightness stands between him and many of the things he claims to want such as freedom, abundance, and joy. He doesn't want to make money because he believes it is immoral to do so. Therefore, he has no way of supporting himself and his family on the outside. Therefore, he has spent most of his life in jail and prison. Even when he bailed out, he made a simple error that put him back in jail within a week.

The problem with the goal of being "right" is that it means everyone else is wrong. It means everything else is wrong. This closes off the opportunity for growth. Being "right" eliminates the possibility that something better may come along. It prevents flexibility and considering new information. When we look for "what works," we realize that what worked yesterday, may no longer work today. Therefore, we are open to new ideas. When we focus on being right, we create significant mental blocks because everything other than our "right" is "wrong" and not open for consideration.

Once something is labeled as "wrong," the only thing left to do to that something is to punish it. Unfortunately, we often label things "wrong" just because they are different, even when trying to solve major problems. All problems are created by a certain line of thinking. To solve the problem, we must think differently than we did when creating the problem. However, if we are always labeling different things as wrong and punishing them, we just perpetuate the same problems. I wonder how long our society will continue to operate in this manner before it destroys itself.

I continue to hear about people being released from jail who have no place to go. They choose jail because it is secure because it gives them three meals a day and a play to stay. In here, they seem normal and well-adjusted because they are secure. On the street, they panic and don't know how to handle life. They struggle with the freedom of choices.

I suspect they struggle so much with choices because they are afraid they'll do something wrong.

Friday January 14, 2011

I received several letters yesterday including one from a best-selling author. This Psychologist/Writer had talked about our situation with our adult children and wanted to lead a media blitz. I was honored with her offer.

I met the Psychologist/Writer in Santa Fe more than a year ago. I was immediately impressed with her openness and willingness to share about her various life experiences. She was drawn to me and we've chatted often since then. On several occasions, she asked me for advice about family issues. After our first conversation, I recognized her name but couldn't place it. When I Googled her name, I was surprised to discover who she was.

The Psychologist/Writer is older than my parents. However, age doesn't slow down her life. She still plays tennis, enjoys social gatherings and jet sets to speaking engagements where she talks about sexual health. She is an example of how to add years to life without aging. I greatly admire her ability to live life to its fullest.

Her book was cutting edge material in the 1980s and millions of people have benefitted from her writing. It opened the way for frank discussions about how sex can be more enjoyable for women and it was criticized for daring to talk openly about the subject. She hated the criticism but she never regretted the explicitness of her book. I've often heard her say that Masters and Johnson wrote about sexuality too but they avoided the criticism because they hid their opinions within vague comments. They knew society wasn't ready for the unedited truth so they wrote obscurely to get the message across in a culture not ready for it. My opinion is that The Psychologist/Writer got the message across that Masters and Johnson didn't clearly communicate.

Her experiences have led her to say our current American system is leaning towards "fascism" because of the need to enforce "rightness" through an authoritarian system. Based on my experiences over the past few weeks, I agree with her diagnosis. I look forward to the opportunity to use this writing to change that so we can once again be a free society.

I also received letters from The Wife, College Friend, and Son Three. I realized that I had become so engrossed in *The Gift of Asher Lev* that I was responding to The Wife as if she was Devorah, Asher's wife. I processed that by reading The Wife's letter. I recognized her loyalty to my message. She does understand who I am and what we believe. Most importantly, she is not Devorah. I no longer feel the distance between us that I felt a couple days ago.

Son Three visited me today. It is the first time I've seen him since the arrest. He and Son Two are not going to shave until we are released. He said they have been told we will either have computers or copies of the files in a week, so I'm thrilled about that. My hope has been that the computers will arrive home before we do so this seems to be a good sign.

Cellmate One is struggling today. I'm not sure why except that he didn't get his indigent pack through commissary last night. Cellmate Two and I observed that Cellmate One's lack on the streets contributes to his territorial behavior in here.

I ordered a priority envelope so I could mail my journal to the office and they could begin typing it. I apparently didn't complete my order form correctly, so I didn't receive my order last night. I have now decided to send my writings, five pages at a time, in the envelopes I've received in the past two commissary orders. By the time I've completed today's writing, there will be thirteen envelopes on the way to the office.

The media continues to contact our family regarding this case. Channel 4 called the house last night and Son Three said they declined comment. I still have mixed feelings about how to use the media in this situation. I need to have a conversation with Substitute Attorney because I'm sure the interviews will help me sell books but I don't want to hurt the case either.

I just finished reading *Into the Wild* by Jon Krakauer. It is about Chris McCandless, a young man who went into the Alaskan Wilderness and died. Ron White does a standup comedy routine about the movie. Otherwise, I hadn't heard the story.

As I read the book, I was struck by how people often become mad at God when a loved one dies. This happened to Chris's family. It was also mentioned in books I previously read. This is common when we see God as a "giant vending machine in the sky" instead of as co-creator with us.

All spiritual writings say that we are Gods. They teach about our creative roles and how those roles intervene with other people's roles to produce situations in which we grow spiritually. Sometimes, this includes death. However, we always control the timing of our death. Sometimes, this is a conscious control. Other times, it is a subconscious or super conscious control, part of the life plan we designed before coming into this version of ourselves.

Without this perspective, bad things are used as excuses to become angry with God, to deny God, to build a barrier to relationship to God. We see God as angry, vengeful, punishing, and full of wrath. Therefore, we handle our own relationships that way and build a culture that is angry, vengeful, punishing, and full of wrath. We innately know that we must model God's behavior. Therefore, whatever we believe about God, we become ourselves. Is it any wonder that religion struggles so much with the concept of a God who loves all, doesn't punish sin, and doesn't want to crush us with fire and brimstone? Because, if God was loving all the time, that would obligate religion to be loving all the time and religions goal is to control, not to love.

The lack of basic education skills of the inmates in here became apparent to me today. I saw it on so many levels it left my head spinning. Some guys can't add or do other simple math skills. Some can't read. Some can't write. To make up for it, they bluster their way through situations by being macho. Since we play a lot of cards, the most macho thing they can do is slam a card on the table when playing it. Then, they complain because the cards are bent and torn.

It really isn't just a lack of basic education skills like math and reading. There is a lack of social and emotional skills. Many inmates become sullen at the tiniest upset to their situation. Today, without reason, one went up to another and started to choke him. There was no harm done but there were fifteen seconds of excitement followed by apologies.

I watched Fighter Pilot firmly tell another guy not to talk about his case because it was a downer to everyone else. Then, Fighter Pilot struggled with his emotions the rest of the night. Cellmate One has been moody all day about commissary trades. This over items that all retail for less than $5.00. Religious Guy goes into emotional funks when he makes mistakes at cards. He covers them by making excuses over silly little things like the cards he receives or the way he sorted them.

Even the staff lacks educational and social skills, especially when speaking to the inmates. They struggle with their communication skills and bluff their way through by raising their voice and using profanities. Their behavior just reinforces the inmates' loud behavior. In addition, the staff either has little consideration for the inmates or purposely creates situations to wake us throughout the night. Crackling walkie-talkies turned up loudly or loud rock music often interrupts sleep.

Another thing the staff does is randomly change TV channels. Every TV in this facility is controlled by one signal. When one CO doesn't like what is on, he or she calls whoever controls the TV and asks them to change channels. There may be twenty-five people watching a show and the channel will change halfway through and everyone will disperse because they don't want to watch the new show. (The only thing that is consistent is sports. If a game is on, it stays on.) I don't know if the channel changing just happens or if they change the channels on purpose, just to mess with the inmates. I wonder if staff ever stops to consider how they change the dynamics of an

235

entire POD (and possibly the entire facility) by changing the TV channel.

The sense of humor with the inmates and staff is childish at best. Crude bathroom humor is about all most understand and if I say anything funny, I have to really back off the sophistication or no one understands it except Cellmate Two. He's one of the smartest guys in here and one of the most compassionate.

We've talked a lot about his life on the outside. I'm impressed with his thoughts about life, relationships, parenting, and work. He is another example of how the system is counterproductive. Cellmate Two works two jobs, supports his children, and is an honest communicator. He learned his lessons from his initial situation. However, his ex-girlfriend learned how to play the legal game and has made his life miserable by filing false reports that have landed him in court on a regular basis and, now, back in jail.

All it takes is a phone call to the authorities and an individual will go to jail. A person is no longer innocent until proven guilty. A person is guilty as charged because he is slightly outside the bounds of normal. One of my clients, The Educational Anarchist, calls it "The Narrowing of Normal." She says society has made the definition of "normal" so narrow that 95% of the population is no longer normal. Therefore, those in power have reason to arrest those 95% if they decide to do so.

The Dumpster Diver continues to make his trashcan surveys. When done, he walks around the POD, tall and skinny with dark hair, his tongue stuck into his left nostril. No one seems bothered by him.

Leprechaun is working hard on becoming a Christian. I see him studying his Bible every day. He is reading other religious material too. He even loaned me a Christian book because he knows I like to read.

While playing cards last night, the conversation turned to sex. I just listened and was surprised when two of the five guys at the table admitted they are virgins. I thought to myself, "There are virgins in the 'perv POD!' I didn't expect that."

Truthfully, I had a lot of preconceived notions about jail and my experience has shattered them. I hear there are violent PODS. I hear there are PODS where the guards sneak heroin and other drugs in for the inmates and drug deals are as common as commissary deals in this POD. I hear that the reason the fire alarms keep going off is because, when inmates smoke, they blow smoke into the vents. However, those haven't been my experiences.

My experience is that people are people wherever they are located. When a group of people live together, a community is formed. Each person within that community has different strengths and weaknesses. Some are intelligent. Some are not so intelligent. Some have social skills. Some lack social skills. I am attracted to some. I am not attracted to others. I choose who I spend time with by sorting in some and sorting out others.

It really isn't much different from life on the outside.

Saturday, January 15, 2011

I awoke this morning feeling "run over by a truck." Even after eating and talking with Daughter One on the phone, the feeling persisted. I wonder if it is because I have lost weight and my body is adjusting.

There is a theory, primarily Buddhist in origins I believe, that says we don't need food to survive. It says there is enough energy in air that we can process the "prana" from it to live. Because of the quality of the food in here, I have been tempted to see if it would work for me. I know examples of other people who have done this. The Buddha did this. More recently, a young man called "The Buddha Boy" lived this way for months. These two individuals lived by sitting under a tree for months without taking in food or water. I don't know of any examples of people who have lived an active life this way.

Daughter One said that lots of people have said they will be at Tuesday's "amended arraignment." In addition, Substitute Attorney said she will see me before then, so the next few days will be interesting. I suspect that part of my feeling today comes from the "What's next?" question in my head/gut. I don't know what an amended arraignment is.

As much as I believe in maintaining Peace of Mind, it isn't something that is automatic for me. When I have the feeling that I have today, I know it is a spiritual/emotional feeling that contributes, possibly causes, the physical heaviness.

It is at these times that I have to go back through the list of reminders. Is this situation out of my control? Yes. Is it pushing me ahead more quickly in areas that would not have happened otherwise? Yes, I'm losing the PITA (pain in the ass) clients. Does this situation qualify then as a miracle? Yes, it is a shortcut in time and space. Is it part of the "Conspiracy for me"? Absolutely, everything is part of this conspiracy. Just the act of writing those questions and answers helps me through this feeling.

Cellmate Two came to the room last night and said, "I picked up this book downstairs for you. It looks like something you'd like."

"What is it?"

"The author is Richard Bach. The book is *One.*"

I smiled. "That's a great book. Thank you. "

Richard Bach was the author The Crush told me about when we reconnected after more than thirty years. I was thrilled to have one of his books to read. In addition, I loved that Cellmate Two had identified the book as something I would like.

I watched an inmate manufacture a washing machine today. He took his clothes, put them in a plastic trash bag, and went to the shower. He put some soap and water in the bag and started sloshing it around. He rinsed them when he was done.

We had our first real fight in here today. Again, it took place while I was in the shower. I missed it completely because it happened outside. Two of the loudest Afro-Americans fought. One ended up with a bloody lip. They'll go to medical and then, on to a different SEG POD, one where they are really segregated.

I chatted with Cellmate Two about Cellmate One's mood. Cellmate Two said it comes from Cellmate One not having coffee. Apparently, Cellmate One's security in here comes from whether or not he has coffee. Addictive behavior thrives off many different stimuli. A person may be addicted to alcohol, drugs, control, caffeine, sex, and even writing I suppose. The substance isn't the issue. The issue is how it affects one's behavior. Does it control you or do you control it?

I just finished reading another novel. This one was an exciting and juicy story that I would not have read anywhere else and yet, it spoke to me, touched my heart, and brought tears to my eyes. I desire to be together with our family. I don't even care what we do, as long as we are together.

Sunday, January 16, 2011

Sleeping without lower body pain has become another of my challenges. If I sleep on my side, it hurts my hip and rubs my bedsore. If I sleep on my back, it hurts my heels. Even when I'm awake, it is difficult to find a comfortable position to sit. All of the chairs are hard plastic. All of the stools are stainless steel. My bunk is the most comfortable but it sags in the middle so sitting is awkward at best.

TFT keeps my back healthy and my lungs clear. There is quite a bit of sickness in this enclosed environment and as long as I work out, I'm able to avoid it. I've modified TFT so that I do the leg lifts on my bunk, I walk around the POD, instead of doing the spins, and I do the other three exercises in an empty spot beside the staircase.

About twenty percent of the inmates do some form of physical exercise. They play hardball, walk laps, and do pushups or some other form of calisthenics.

Now that the holiday season is over, a turnover of inmates has started. Some inmates go to prison, some go home, some go to other PODs. New inmates come in. Southern Boy arrived yesterday. He is a big redhead man with a deep southern accent, originally from Alabama. He has charges there and Alabama has ten days to come get him or he can walk. He was drawn to Fighter Pilot's table yesterday, probably because it's a "white table" and since he is from the south, he is prejudiced against anyone with skin darker than his.

I've noticed an increased tension in the POD over the last forty-eight hours. This comes from a combination of new inmates and the fact that court is in full swing after the holidays so other inmates are facing charges. When people are uneducated about what they're facing, it is easy to feel like a victim, to feel unappreciated, to feel taken advantage of. The legal system causes inmates to feel that way. Then, when staff does anything to mess with us like closing all doors when we're out of the cells, randomly changing TV channels, and screaming profanities at us, it only enhances those feelings. I'm surprised I haven't witnessed more violence in here.

Cellmate One has overcome his moodiness and is communicating with us again. All it took was some coffee.

As I read Richard Bach's *One*, I'm reminded of how our current religious, government, and social systems discourage us from pursuing our highest ideals. This is done through establishing systems designed to maintain the status quo rather than bring improvement to our world. Once government becomes involved in large businesses such as medicine, education, the military, and corrections, it produces a society that inbreeds itself into destruction. On the surface, these systems appear to work because they create employment opportunities while producing results. Unfortunately, these job opportunities are limited and the results are mediocre. This creates a society that appears to move forward when it is actually spiraling backwards. Those in power know that if true change happens, they will have to change and they may lose power. Instead, if they can postpone change, they can remain in their positions of expertise and power.

In fairness to the large government entities and the related businesses, I understand the obstacles to change. For example, a little jet ski is flexible on the water and can change direction quickly. However, a large ship takes significant time to change direction. The pure bulk of the government system makes change a slow process. Of course, if the large ship is heading for dangerous rocks, it would still be wise to initiate a direction change if the ship if going to stay afloat. I can think of many areas where change is necessary if we are going to pursue our highest ideals.

One area is medicine. The basis of many western medicine practices isn't the health of the patient. It is the avoidance of medical lawsuits while creating repeat business by use of prescription drugs approved by the government. If a healing path doesn't fit within the government mandates for health, the practitioner must work secretly or take his practice to another country. The evidence and results are secondary considerations to the government agencies. The primary consideration is control. A medical professional often must choose between doing what is best for the patient and submitting to government regulation. The government's path for a new medicine is so difficult that terminal patients often have to go to another county or fight long court battles to receive a new and effective treatment.

Another area is education. Education decisions are controlled by bureaucrats who often have worked in a government and political environment all their careers. Therefore, education isn't the first priority for teachers. Instead, educators are more concerned with keeping their jobs, tenure, and personal financial security. Students are not taught how to think for themselves and develop personal freedom because their educational preparation is to work jobs, just like their teachers, so they can be "Just Over Broke." Any educator who steps outside the norm and encourages creative thinking often does so at the risk of losing her job.

One goal of the education system is to create adults that fit well into government positions, including military jobs, where all a person has to do is "follow orders." Following orders is much easier than thinking for oneself and our current society is streamlined to teach us to follow orders. This discourages creative thinking, the use of intuition, and the evolving of our society. It produces weak leadership because leaders don't have to think through their decisions, they can just get people to do things "because I said so."

This makes it easy for the military to train its members to kill people and break things. The government justifies this training and the related orders through "proving" that some individual, group, or county *deserves* punishment. This mental training then becomes so dominant that those people trained by our government to kill people and break things often do the same acts outside of government orders. At this point, they may be arrested and punished for doing what they were trained to do.

This punishment philosophy is not limited to the military. It is so prevalent within our culture that it dominates our current way of life. As citizens see the punishment mentality of those in charge, each person begins to see himself as a punisher, looking for an opportunity to take down the next person who doesn't appear "normal." This is especially troubling when we realize that normal has changed from meaning "the majority of the population" to meaning "anyone who gets outside of the bland, follow-the-leader mentality encouraged in our society." Since our current system has narrowed normal, it discourages creative thinking because those thoughts may lead to change and the disruption of the current power system, where each person feels a need to punish anyone who thinks differently.

As the United States government continues to expand its control over various industries, this philosophy continues to expand. Over the past few years, the government expanded its control by bailing out the banking and auto manufacturing industries. The public complained at length about using taxpayer dollars to assist private business. These complaints, however valid, served as smokescreens to divert attention from what was really taking place. The bailouts came at a huge loss of freedom for these two industries. In exchange for the bailout money, the banking and auto manufacturing industries gave the government significant control. This control was important to the government because these two industries are directly tied to two of the government's greatest cash cows: illegal drugs and oil.

The connection between oil and autos is obvious. The connection between illegal drugs and banking may not be so obvious until one understands the connection between the success of drug enforcement laws and the recent banking crisis. According to Antonio Maria Costa, the head of the U.N. Office on Drugs and Crime, more than three hundred fifty billion dollars from the illegal drug trade was funneled to banks between 2007 and 2009. These funds kept the global financial system from collapsing.

The United States government purposely inflates the price of oil by preventing the harvesting of American oil and squashing the use of new technologies. Environmental concerns are used to prevent oil harvesting in American. There is speculation that the recent oil spill in the Gulf of Mexico was orchestrated to allow the government to pass legislation that further hinders harvesting abundant American oil. These actions ensure America's reliance on oil from the Middle East where instability can drive up oil prices, sometimes overnight. In addition, protecting the Middle Eastern oil fields provides justification for a United State Military presence in that area, in case someone there needs to be punished through military action.

Meanwhile, new technology already exists that could replace current gasoline engines without compromising power. I know of at least three people who have created such technology. Each was approached by oil company executives and given "an offer they could not refuse" to sell their technology. I talked with one such gentleman personally when he came to me to discuss tax planning strategy for the funds he was about to receive.

The premeditated inflation of oil prices produces significant profits for oil companies. Many of these profits are used to benefit powerful politicians indirectly through fuel taxes and directly through campaign contributions so the government has a motivation to make sure the oil business is profitable. If the automobile industry had collapsed, the oil business would have gone with it, creating a significant financial crunch for our government.

This same thinking carries over to illegal drugs. The United States government artificially inflated the price by preventing the legality of certain drugs. Testimony from the Iran Contra hearings clearly indicated that the CIA used drug money to supplement the money it received from the Federal Budget. This allowed the CIA to use the full weight of the federal government to protect cooperative drug dealers while arresting those who did not cooperate. In addition, this allowed the government the power to regulate the supply of illegal drugs coming into the country. "Supply and demand" economic theory says that if you can control the supply of a highly demanded product, you can control the price. Many experts believe this government practice continues today.

The government makes money through illegal drugs in at least two ways: first, the CIA makes money as the drugs come into the United States. Second, once the drugs are in the United States, the federal, state, and local law enforcement agencies pursue traffickers, dealers, and users. The punishment philosophy flourishes as American jails are flooded with those arrested for drug offenses. Meanwhile, a large number of government employees have justification for their jobs and the related salaries paid by tax dollars.

Of course, the dollars created through the illegal drug trade eventually end up in a bank. It is interesting to note that recent news stories show that the banks most likely to benefit from the receipt of drug money are the same banks bailed out by the United States government. Since banks are required to report suspected drug-related transactions, it makes sense that part of the agreement between the government and the banks includes allowing drug money to flow through these banks without prosecution. Therefore, the government must make sure those banks stay open so they have a channel for handling the drug money.

The government not only encourages punishment. It creates situations where it must punish people to insure job security. As a local politician told me last summer, "It is a case of politicians creating a problem so they have something to solve." Punishment is used to maintain control of others and to avoid change. Government is the largest perpetrator of this technique and, because it is so prevalent, individuals have been brainwashed to use this same technique without regard for the consequences. We love to find fault with someone else, talk about what they did and what type of punishment they should receive.

I am not judging this system. I'm only observing that our tendency as human beings is to keep working within an old system, even when it no longer produces the desired results. If a new medical procedure can save lives, why is there opposition to using it? If creative thinking helps solve a significant problem, why is there opposition to out-of-the-box thinking? If military battles don't produce peace, then why continue to fight them? If punishment doesn't change behavior, then why punish?

The answer is obvious. We would rather maintain the old than change to the new. This is especially true at the government level. And, since more than a third of the United States population is supported by tax dollars, either through employment or welfare, individuals see no need to initiate change, even when the current system doesn't work.

This produces a society where change , at best, will cost a person his precious job, where he works to be Just Over Broke, or, at worst, be labeled illegal and subject the person to punishment. The mindset produced within this type of society causes people to play "not to lose" instead of playing "to win." Innovative businesses must hire a team of legal experts and paper pushers to document their practices, in case someone chooses to sue them just because they are doing things differently. This practice slows our society's evolution and creates a generation of defensive people.

Government maintains control through the threat of punishment, while doing things that would be illegal if a citizen did them. Individuals become afraid to think creatively, work productively, and promote positive change. The few who desire to initiate change feel like victims in a corrupted system doing things we don't want to do because we're afraid to change the system.

I can write much about this topic because I recognize the resistance to change in my own life. Even though I attempted to follow my intuition and initiate positive change, I was choosing other things over my highest ideals. I was keeping clients I didn't want to keep. I was doing tasks I didn't want to do. I didn't want to lose any opportunity to make money. I didn't want to disappoint other people. I was playing "not to lose," instead of playing "to win."

I had cluttered my life with so many great business opportunities that I was avoiding the freedom of everything life had to offer. I had created my own secure jail of chasing money for money's sake. I was working for people who didn't appreciate the value of my services. They complained every

251

time they got an invoice and tried to figure out a way to get something for nothing.

Now, those clients have judged me and, in their mind, punished me by exiting my life. The clients who appreciate me and see my value are staying, giving me work to do, even while I am in jail. I see that with the difficult clients removed from my life, I can pursue my highest ideals and serve the clients who really appreciate me. I see that as one of the reasons I needed to experience my current situation.

Like I say in my Law of Abundance Seminar, I can go gently, without resistance, or I can resist and let the pressure build up until it explodes. My arrest was an explosion within my business. I didn't know I was resisting. However, the circumstances say otherwise. If the explosion took place, I was resisting.

God was telling me to unclutter my business and I couldn't do it on my own so God helped me by orchestrating this situation. I can't think of a faster way for me to go through transition. Crisis always initiates a major transition. It always clarifies. In my case, it clarified the roles of the people in my life.

We sometimes perceive crisis and transition as a punishment. It isn't. I'm not being punished. The clients moving away from me are not being punished. In fact, no one is being punished in this situation. We're being moved into the next thing and this "crisis" is the beginning of the transition.

This isn't an "us versus them" thing. In spite of each person's various strengths and weaknesses, we are all connected. Living in jail clearly shows me that people are people in any society, large or small. Jail, like life on the outside, has multiple elements. People are old, young, and everything in between. They are black, white, and everything in between. Some have one type of intelligence; some have another type. Some communicate clearly, some use more difficult forms of communication. Some are wealthy, some are not. Because of this experience, I will never judge people in jail as criminals who deserve to be punished because inmates are part of the one, part of the all. I will never judge people anywhere as those who need to be punished because everyone is part of the one, part of the all. If we are to live peacefully, we must know that, see that, and accept it, especially during times we perceive as crisis.

"Hatred is love without the facts."

Richard Bach

Isn't it amazing to consider that when someone understands the truth behind hate, it turns to love? Yes, everything is an act of love or a cry for love. When I see what we perceive as an act of hate, can I look closer and find the love? When I hate someone, am I willing to get more facts so I can turn that hate into love?

When I see the bum on the street corner, do I hate him? Or, do I realize that being a bum is his chosen profession? Do I see the courage it takes to stand on a corner, while risking arrest and snide comments, in the hopes of collecting enough money to eat tonight? Do I take the time to hand him a five dollar bill and see the tears of joy in his eyes as he tells me, "Thank you, I can eat a full meal tonight."

"What if everybody everywhere is some aspect of who we are and we're some aspect of them? How will that change the way we live?"

Richard Bach

I think that would significantly change the way we live. I know that my ranting about our current society was really a rant about myself. When I go back and read the previous pages, I know that God orchestrated all of those things for my benefit and for the benefit of every person affected by this situation. Every CO, every fellow inmate, every family member, every friend, and every client gained clarity about his or her life in some way. Those who are angry at me are angry with themselves. Those who feel sorry for me feel sorry for themselves. Those who love and accept me love and accept themselves.

Reading Bach's writing always increases the awareness of my unlimited ability, of mankind's unlimited ability and capacity to love without judging. Do I understand that the person who hates me doesn't know himself, so he doesn't know me? He doesn't recognize that he and I share aspects of one another and that, as he hates me, he hates himself. In fact, he can only hate me because he hates himself. He judges me so harshly because he judges himself so harshly and I remind him of himself. Once he comes to love himself, he will love me. However, his religion tells him he is a sinner that needs to be punished. His society tells him that if he does something wrong, he needs to be punished. He innately knows this system doesn't work so an internal conflict rages within his heart. Therefore, he

254

looks for ways to resolve this internal conflict by initiating an external conflict so, he can play it out and gain understanding.

I truly want to understand how to love all people. Therefore, this external conflict is with me so I can process the situation and recognize the part of me in him that wants to punish, embrace it, and change it to love. I learn to change hate to love by accepting the fact that I am an aspect of each person in my life and each person in my life is an aspect of me. Jail allows me the time to process this without wildly running around in pursuit of other things.

I have worried about the time wasted while in here and then, I am reminded that time cannot be wasted. In fact, according to Einstein, it may not even be real.

"For us believing physicists, the distinction between past, present, and future is only an illusion, even if it is a stubborn one."

Albert Einstein

I remember that time is just a dimension that keeps everything from happening at one time. It is an illusionary tool used to allow humans to experience sequential processes. Einstein knew this, proved this, and lived within the illusion. As I think about this great scientist and the impact he had on our world, I'm reminded that all answers are within. I'm reminded that each person has the ability to go within, connect to God, the all-knowing being, and get whatever answers he needs. Since God resides outside the t me dimension, when I make this connection with God, I can connect with any aspect of God that I need from the past, present or future. If I need an answer from Einstein, I can connect with the Einstein aspect of God. If I need an answer from Abraham Lincoln, I can connect with the Abraham Lincoln aspect of God. If I need an answer from some yet unknown future genius, I can connect with that future, unknown genius aspect of God too.

In other words, for every question I have, I can find the answer. The answer is always there, I just have to ask and then find that part of me that knows by connecting with that aspect of God, of me, that knows. Yes, a full day of lockdown while reading Richard Bach was a pleasant way to spend the day.

We were allowed out of our cells at 4 PM and the tension continued. The past few days I've smelled smoke – something different from burnt popcorn. Microwave popcorn is available through commissary. However, most of the inmates can't cook it without burning it so everyone knows what burnt popcorn smells like. Cellmate One knows how to cook it without burning it so I share my popcorn with him. I provide the popcorn. He cooks it.

My cellmates say the smoke I smell is someone smoking tobacco. This is a smoke-free facility so that's a no-no. Yesterday's CO noticed but didn't care. Tonight's CO is C. He is a straight, by-the-book CO who loves to use the "F word' when he talks to us.

He smelled the smoke as soon as we came out of our cells after afternoon lockdown. I watched him look around and check the microwave for burning popcorn. When he didn't find burning popcorn, he called us to Command Call. I could see the apprehension on faces. Everyone knew what was going to happen and everyone moved quickly to stand with hands behind our backs outside our cells. As soon as there was silence, C broke it.

"Who's fucking smoking shit on my shift? Who's got the balls to man up and admit it?"

No one spoke. No one moved except for C as he sat in his chair at the CO's station and attempted to look each inmate in the eye.

"I'll lock you down and turn this fucking place upside down."

Again, there were no confessions. C realized his questions would go unanswered. He sighed.

"Ok, you just lost an hour. Lockdown is at seven. You're clear."

C's relief for his break arrived and he was anxious to leave. He wanted to punish the smoker. Since he couldn't, he would punish all of us. It was as natural as breathing to him.

Some inmates went back to NFL game on the tube. I went downstairs to play cards with Fighter Pilot, Religious Guy and Southern Boy while we waited for dinner to arrive.

Just as C started to leave the POD for his break, I heard scuffling on the top tier.

A couple of inmates yelled C's name. I ignored them. Then, I heard something else, the sounds of flesh on flesh.

"POW! SMACK!"

I looked up from my Rummy hand to see two inmates squaring off. A dark skinned inmate and a Native American were going after one another at the top of the stairs. At first, I was concerned they would tumble down the metal staircase. I could imagine the pain and injuries as skin and bones tumbled into the metal railings and steps. Those concerns left, to be replaced by new ones as the fight evolved into a beating.

The dark skinned inmate pounded the Native as the Native retreated towards the showers. Now, I was concerned that they would slide and fall on the water and slam into the tile walls and barriers.

C and his relief called for backup on their radios as they ran up the stairs, mace pulled. I stayed in my seat, wanting to avoid the mace and hoping no more damage would be done. I couldn't remember the last time I had witnessed a fight that wasn't part of a sporting event or otherwise staged.

"Stop it!"

"NOW!"

The beating continued.

C pulled the dark skinned inmate away while his relief sprayed mace towards the Native. The Native ducked and I watched the spray of mace hit one of the two guys in the shower.

I sighed. The fight was over. However, the relief still had a need to punish someone. Did he act out of fear? Did he act because he had a need to control someone else? Did he not understand that the humidity from the showers would elevate the effect of the mace and bring discomfort to those not involved in the fight, standing naked in the shower stall? I could almost understand his need to punish the Native. However, now, he was punishing people not involved in the fight.

The Sergeant and another staff member ran into the POD. Their eyes were wide with fear as they ran up the stairs screaming, "Lock this POD down!"

I pulled my shirt over my nose and walked up the stairs. I held my breath as I went by the shower area and was able to get to my cell without experiencing more than mild discomfort from the mace. I wanted to ball up on my bunk and just think, think about everything I had written this afternoon, think about our insatiable need to punish others, think about why we feel the need to punish others.

Instead, I watched as the staff escorted the fighters down the steps and into the sally port, on the way to medical. I knew medical would patch them up and they would go to another segregation POD where they wouldn't have the freedoms available to us in SEG 1. We would have two less inmates in our POD tonight. As a result, we would receive dinner through our chuck doors and eat in our cells.

Cellmate Two had watched the fight develop and he told me and Cellmate One what happened. The Native was the one smoking and the dark skinned inmate was angry with him because he had cost us free time. He decided it was time to "make him pay" and punish him for his actions. I listened in awed amazement as I recognized that I had just seen what I spent the afternoon writing about. Our system of punishment was so habitual that every moment of our brief time outside the cell was filled with punishment.

The CO punished because someone was smoking. One inmate punished another because he was smoking. The staff sprayed mace on a fighter and a guy taking a shower because of the fight. The staff then took the two fighters to medical and on to a POD with more stringent segregation standards. Every act was an act of punishment. Would people still smoke? Yes. Would people still fight? Yes. Would punishment change

259

behaviors? No. Would people still punish? Yes. Is insanity doing the same thing over and over again expecting different results?

It is interesting to me that on the day I finally get my hands on a spiritual book and am reminded of how everybody is some aspect of me, that I experience the most troublesome day in here. Do I want to smoke? Do I want to fight? Do I want to be sprayed with mace? Do I want to punish? Does an alternate reality of me want to do these things?

Monday, January 17, 2011

After several days of tension, two fights in two days, and the removal of four of the most volatile people from the POD, I thought today would be less tense. If anything, the tension is thicker, much thicker. Today's CO, T, is an attractive young Hispanic woman that Fighter Pilot calls "prune face" because of how her pulled-back hair makes her face look tight, so tight it is going to explode.

T runs a tight POD, and often does little things to increase tension, such as locking us out of the cells, locking down the POD for minor infractions, and not turning on the TV. She started the day by shaking down some cells to look for contraband, probably tobacco, before calling us to command call for meds. Then she closed all cell doors once we were out of the cells for lunch. They aren't enough tables for everyone to have a place to eat, so most inmates eat in the cells. Today, they ate on the floor.

The combination of the residual tension and T's methods of operation have created an air of unease that is greater today than any day I've been at MDC. Today is a good day to practice the "Emissary of Peace Meditation." With this meditation, I breathe in the tension of the surroundings. I feel that energy and recognize that it is just energy. Of course, if I perceive the energy as tension, that means I've applied a filter to the energy. In this case, it is a filter of tension.

As I feel this energy and allow it to reside within me, I own it. I embrace it. I do not fight it. I become it. What I resist persists. What I embrace, I can change. Once that energy becomes me and I become it, I can remove the tension filter. Since I feel tension in the survival or root chakra, I see the ball of energy residing in that location. Because this is my energy and I've embraced it, I can do whatever I want with it, so I remove the tension filter and the energy becomes lighter. Now, it is free to become love and I visualize it moving up my body into the heart chakra. By the time it arrives there, the pure, unfiltered energy is transformed. I started with energy, filtered as tension. I transformed it to pure energy, allowed it to become lighter, move into my heart and become love.

I feel the love. I own it. I allow it to fill my being. Then, as I connect to God through the chakras in my forehead and at the top of my head, I breathe out love, spreading it to the Universe and my immediate surroundings. Yes, it is a good day to practice this.

Today was a beautiful clear day and I saw several crows, each flying higher and higher. They reminded me of my longing to be home, serving others, enjoying my friends and family. I believe their message to me is to remain without attachment to results, loving wherever I am, whomever I'm with. By doing this, I may experience higher and higher attributes of freedom no matter where my physical body is located.

I chatted with My Helper today. She said Substitute Attorney is optimistic about The Wife and I being released this week.

Cellmate One and I talked about Dumpster Diver. I was wrong about what he is doing in the trashcans. He is not pulling out brightly colored paper. Instead, he is filling every bag in the trashcan so that no space is wasted. The items he pulls out of the trash, he flattens so that more of them will fit in each bag and the trash can doesn't have to be emptied as often.

I chuckled when I realized that Cellmate One would understand Dumpster Diver's behavior. Both of them have obsessive compulsive tendencies when it comes to cleanliness. Suddenly, I could see the connection between the two men and understand why each person was in here. Most of society would be uncomfortable with each person, so removing them from society is the way to solve this issue. The charges against each person served as excuses to do so. My situation felt similar. Were The Wife and I in jail because we were criminals or because people were uncomfortable with us?

I thought last night's fight resolved the smoking and tobacco issue. After all, the perpetrator had been beaten by a fellow inmate, sprayed with mace by a staff member, removed from our GP POD and sent to a true SEG POD. What I didn't take into consideration was the Sergeant's need to participate in the punishment. He came into the POD tonight and said that if the tobacco doesn't show up on the COs desk, we'll be locked down until it does. From what I hear, the remaining tobacco was quickly flushed when the Native left the POD. Therefore, there is no tobacco to put on the COs desk. I guess someone will have to smuggle some into the POD to meet the Sergeant's demands.

Substitute Attorney visited me today, gave me a copy of the indictment, and the legal code for my case. In addition, she explained the hundreds of years I could serve if I'm found guilty on all counts. She encouraged me to read the charges, review the code, and figure out how to defend myself. She said she will do everything she can to get us out tomorrow so we can prepare for trial. Trial preparation is easier on the outside than the inside.

She told me all of this while she was shaking. It wasn't cold in the POD. In fact, it was warm. Therefore, I assumed Substitute Attorney was nervous about something related to my case. Was it the charges? Was she afraid of failing tomorrow? Was she being threatened somehow by this situation? I had heard through the grapevine that she lost her judgeship. One person said she was fired. Another said she resigned. I had not asked her about it. Now, I wondered if she was projecting her situation onto my situation. I wasn't planning to change attorneys. However, I sensed that I might have that opportunity in the future.

Throughout my meeting with Substitute Attorney, my heart calmly spoke to me, telling me to listen to her counsel and to know that this case would be different from the norm. It told me to look for the inconsistencies in the indictment, not to attach to results, to trust. The more my heart spoke to me, the more I relaxed.

I hope I sleep well tonight. Court is tomorrow.

Tuesday, January 18, 2011

I slept peacefully throughout the night. Now, I have showered, shaved, and eaten breakfast and I wait for a staff member to escort me to transportation so I can go to court.

The message I keep receiving about today is that I can trust the result, whatever it is. Do I want to be released? Absolutely. Is my heart set on that? Am I attached to it? Yes, a little bit. However, I also understand that God will do what is best for me today.

It's interesting to watch myself go through this process. I'm a spectator of an elaborate production. I can see nothing else but the drama of my life – this life in jail – and watch it play out as I escape from everything outside.

I'm reminded that we step into theatres to watch a drama, a comedy, a romance. We completely leave behind everything outside those four walls for the time we're in the theatre. Nothing else matters except what takes place on the stage or the screen. We live and breathe with the actors. We cry when they cry. We thrill when they are thrilled. We ride those emotions. Then, when the stage darkens, the screen goes to black, we walk outside with our emotions refreshed, our hearts recharged, and we go back to life, remembering the lessons from the drama.

Jail is as the production, except I am one of the characters, placed inside the drama, the four walls of the theatre. I am the actor and the audience, the participant and the viewer. I merge with myself until I can no longer tell which role I play and then I separate again.

Life is jail. Jail is life. I become the actor, the viewer, the producer, the director. I move from role to role, merging, shifting, changing until I merge back into God, my lessons learned, my experience complete.

This is the cycle of life. Some of us do this through jail time. Others do it through hospital stays, serious illnesses and accidents, financial disasters, or other outrageous events. We face the experience; we move on, we become richer. We grow softly strong in cracked places.

Court was quick today. Everyone played their roles. Substitute Attorney argued her arguments. The judge did his judging. The TV cameramen recorded their tape. The guards guarded us. The audience, consisting of a courtroom full of friends and family, supported us. The bonds lowered from $500,000 cash to $100,000 cash or surety.

As soon as my hearing was over, I was escorted to a holding cell, where I signed my conditions of release and waited for transportation back to MDC. I ran numbers. I knew that some bailsmen would take a 3% down payment if we agreed to make payments on the balance. I thought we had that amount of money so maybe we could get out in the next few days. I relaxed into that without attaching to the results.

I arrived at MDC, waited patiently as I went through holding, had my shackles and handcuffs removed, was given my sack lunch, and escorted back to the POD. After eating my lunch, I decided to call Daughter One and see if she and

Substitute Attorney had come up with the same numbers I had come up with to get us out of jail.

"Hi sweetie. What's up?"

"Hi Daddy. We're writing checks and signing paperwork so we can see you tonight."

"Really?"

"Yeah, I have 5, Friend One has 10, Friend Two has 5"

"Wow! You mean...." My vision blurred and I couldn't finish the sentence.

"Oh Daddy, don't cry"

From the background, "Is he crying?"

"Our bail is paid?"

"Yes, Daddy. We want you home."

I felt the credits roll. As the stage darkened, I could no longer tell if I was the audience or the actor, the producer or the director. As the screen went to black, my eyes continued to blur and I felt my emotions refresh, my heart recharge. In a few hours, I would walk outside and go back to life, remembering the lessons from the drama.

I rejoiced in that I had grown softly strong in cracked places.

I also knew the biggest growth was yet to come.

Notes About the Author

Matthew C. Cox grew up the only child of a conservative family in the foothills of Virginia. He was raised under the watchful and protective eyes of loving Christian parents who wanted him to grow up and get a steady job so he could take proper care of the family he would inevitably have. He was encouraged to pursue work in the ministry.

He graduated from East Carolina University, in North Carolina, with a degree in Music Education and quickly determined he had no interest in working for the public school system so he used his education to teach private music lessons, primarily to home schooled children. In addition, he taught Bible Studies, led youth groups, was involved in street ministry, and played in bands that proclaimed what he believed to be the truth of the Gospel.

Shortly after graduation from college, Matthew attended a seminar that would help him discover and begin to shape his Life Purpose: fifty people in three generations to make a positive impact in the world, ultimately to help bring world peace. Within a few months of reaching this understanding, he met the woman he would marry. Together, they started their family and soon moved to the mountains of New Mexico. They noticed life was a different in New Mexico than in North Carolina. They attended seminars and read a wide variety books in an attempt to learn why the atmosphere was so different in New Mexico.

During this search, Matthew began to question everything he had been taught and had in turn devoutly taught to others. He recognized that his religion, which claimed to give Peace of Mind, didn't work for that purpose. He observed that others practicing his religion didn't experience Peace of Mind either. After eight years of questioning and searching, he developed a belief system that was different from what he learned as a child. In fact, he was afraid to share it outside of his family because it was so different from anything he had ever heard before.

At that time, a friend gave him a stack of books that included Neal Donald Walsch's *Conversations with God.* These writings confirmed the conclusions Matthew had made during his journey and gave him the courage to begin his own writing. He documented his journey to Peace of Mind in his first book, *Living the Southwest Lifestyle.*

As his family grew, Matthew experienced an unmatched life of peace and harmony. He, his wife, their children, and their children's partners and children worked together, played together, and lived within a few miles of each other. Matthew had found a belief system that worked for him and he worked towards becoming recognized worldwide as an expert on Peace of Mind.

Of course, having Peace of Mind in peaceful circumstance is easy. An expert must know that Peace of Mind is possible in every circumstance, including the loss of family, home, business, reputation, and the fulfillment of one's Life Purpose. *Growing Softly Stronger in the Cracked Places* is Matthew's story of how he discovered whether his belief system would bring Peace of Mind in some of life's direst circumstances.

Coming Soon!

More Growing Softly Stronger in the Cracked Places will be released in late 2011 or early 2012. To be notified of the final release date, please visit

www.softlystronger.com

and click on the *More Softly Stronger* link.

Another Book by Matthew C. Cox

Living the Southwest Lifestyle
(visit www.ltswls.com)

The Peace of Mind Training Institute

Throughout this novel, I mention my work with The Peace of Mind Training Institute. This is a real tax-exempt organization that exists for the purpose of training people how to have and maintain Peace of Mind. It teaches the philosophy that I used within this novel to maintain Peace of Mind during my time incarcerated. You may learn more about this organization by visiting www.PeaceOfMindTrainingInstitute.com.